Complete Edition

The Politics Of Money

Written By

Gregory Mannarino

The Politics Of Money

ISBN: 978-1-300-07698-8

Friends, this book comprises my most important work and is an assembly of my previously published works. I have also taken the liberty to expand on some of these topics as well as to bring this edition up to date.

There are many who believe that the times which lie ahead are uncertain, but this line of thinking is terribly flawed. The current global economic path has set the stage for a financial future which is literally written in stone. In fact think of it this way, a fiscal wrecking ball is hurling directly at you at this very moment and it is unstoppable. But facing this reality head on allows you to be able to make critical decisions now which will greatly affect your future financial well being. What must be understood by you the reader is this, we are at a paradox, a crossroads if you will, one which will certainly leave a vast majority of people destitute and desperate while others will prosper greatly. History has demonstrated that it is at times like these in which fortunes are made and also lost.

Gregory Mannarino

Contents

*"The most successful person on the Earth
is the one who creates their own path."*

Introduction

The U.S. Economy Is The Biggest Rigged Game In The History Of The World

Hi everybody it's me Gregory Mannarino, how are you today? For the many thousands of you worldwide who follow my daily YouTube blog you hear me start each video segment in that same manner, so why stop there? As a further introduction for those of you who are not familiar with who I am and what I do, please allow me to tell you a little about myself. I began my financial career on Wall Street working for the securities and trading arm of the now defunct Bear Stearns. I also hold a medical degree and practice clinical medicine. As an undergraduate I studied finance, economics, and the natural sciences. I served as a commissioned officer in the United States Naval Reserve Medical Service Corps, having attained the rank of lieutenant. I also enjoy studying military tactics and strategy. I Have also been involved with the gaming industry, having written a book on casino blackjack strategies. My experience with Wall Street trading, penchant for economics, finance, and military tactics, has provided me with a unique and compelling perspective into the machinations involved.

For me understanding what makes something tick has always been fascinating. Human behavior as well. Human psychology plays an enormous role in gaming as well as economics. In fact what most people fail to realize is that consumer sentiment, which is the commonly used term for consumer "psyche," is the main driver involved in equity trading as well as economics. Fundamental or technical factors involving the overall markets play a back seat role to human perception in determining an asset's price, where the overall market is headed, and even whether an economy thrives or collapses. The science of economics is not a straight forward idea, and in many ways it is like the practice of medicine in that the expected outcome my be different than the actual result. Economies or more specifically how an economy is run is massively influenced by human conceptualization, and today more than any other time history with the merger of government and corporate entity's here in the United States perception by the American people is everything.

8

My purpose in writing this book is not to bury you with statistics and numbers with multiple zeros behind them so you can go ooh and ah while at the same time filling up blank pieces of paper. All of the numbers and statistics involved are easily discoverable and can be found in virtually all of the other books written involving the understanding of our economy. My point here is to try and raise people's awareness as to the human side of this super game.

Question: Why is it so important to know how to play this game?

Answer: Because every citizen of every country in the world is forced to participate in this game, and play it.

This is no ordinary Las Vegas casino where all you can lose is your cash. No, in this global casino people are losing their lives. At this point in time on every corner of the world we are witnessing increasing social unrest and political strife. These things are not only going to be growing much worse in their scope, size, and in their violence over the next few years, but they are coming right to your front door. There is great change taking place everywhere in the world, and an enormous amount of effort is being put into causing the people of the western world, especially the United States, to believe they are isolated from these problems. Not only is this a complete falsehood, but in my opinion it is criminal for those who have been voted into office by the American people and have had our trust placed in them to go along with this charade, for they are well aware that a monster is headed our way. A financial wave of destruction is coming which is going to shake the foundation of our beloved country the likes of which nightmares could not even duplicate. Still where is their warning? It would seem that our policymakers are naive to all this, however they are fully cognizant of these things . It would also seem that our policymakers are just overly concerned with staying in office, but this as well is not what it seems. For some the root cause of these things remains elusive, but there is only one clear answer.

Here Is Where This All Begins

This macroeconomic super game for which you are a direct participant has rules, and I am going to explain clearly what the rules are. I will detail for you where the dangers lie, and I will show you who the major players are. But most importantly I am going to teach you how to win.

It must be understood that you cannot win this game by beating the major players of which there are three, as they cannot be beaten. The only way you can win this game is by having a clear understanding of how this game is going to play out, and that is the sole reason why I wrote this book. I suppose the real question is this, are you willing to fight for your life? Your survival is on the line in this game, so I hope you have got what it takes to win. You can think of this book as a survival manual.

In any game, project, investment, etc. you cannot simply "fly by the seat of your pants" so to speak and just hope for the best, understand that there are people on the other side of the equation who are hoping you do just that. They are hoping you make critical mistakes, of which they can capitalize upon. It is crucial to understand that you must be aware of how decisions you make at any given moment are going to affect you in the long run. Too many people just live in the moment which is nice for that brief period of time, but you have to understand and be aware of the ramifications of your actions or inaction for that matter. Newtons 3rd physical law dictates: *every action has an equal and opposite reaction.* But what would happen if inaction from an animate being leads to misfortune? Does that mean that an action had actually taken place? Sir Newton seems to suggest that inaction would have no reaction, so are human beings immune from physical laws? More on this concept later on.

Understanding The Game

This economic super game is global, but because the United States is the biggest economy of them all most of the rules begin here. In the course of events, by the time most people figure out what is going on it is already way too late. A vast majority of the time when the general public acts on a opportunity the situation has already played out or is close to conclusion. The converse is also true as people also tend to react to danger way too late, and these scenarios have been repeated countless times throughout history with consistently bad outcomes. How many times have you heard someone say, "Wow I wish I would have got in on that sooner, I would be rich today."? Or how about this, "I bought my house at the market peak, and now the value of my house has plummeted!" What I want to convey to you is a sense of urgency. We are at a precipice, a major economic tectonic shift of epic proportions is just beyond the horizon and there is no way to stop it from coming right at you. The urgency is this: you can choose to survive it or not. It is my hope that you choose to survive.

Please do not misunderstand me, this macroeconomic monster which is evolving as you are reading this sentence is going to unleash horror upon the human race, and in several parts of the world it has already begun. Today right in the midst of this developing global economic crisis, in direct response to it point of fact, there is an opportunity for people to become massively wealthy, and this is the paradox. The vast majority of the general population of not just the United States, but the world are going to be left destitute, and many will continue to die. But some like you, simply because you are reading this book right now have the opportunity of a lifetime. Throughout history it is at times like these when fortunes are made, and also lost. Here in the United States at this time it would seem to most that things are not so bad, unless you are one of those who cannot find a job. But for those of us who are working you may look around and say "Hey, I am getting by, the stock markets seem to be doing well, real estate prices are stabilizing, sure the price of things seem to have risen a but I can still afford to feed my family."

If that is the case you should consider yourself fortunate because what is not blatantly obvious is this, there are over 44 million people in America right now receiving food stamps. To put this into a perspective for you, this means is if we were now living during the time of the Great Depression these same people would be standing on bread lines and waiting in soup kitchens for food. Because people have access to food stamps there are no "visual" bread lines but they still exist. If food stamps were not available the bread lines of today would be in seen in every city of every state in the Union, with people standing in lines many city blocks long. What you also would not see are the true numbers regarding unemployment and inflation, which our government manipulates with fancy business techniques. The true numbers regarding both unemployment and inflation have been worked in half via fancy and deliberately misleading math and realistically the true unemployed numbers are near Great Depression levels. What you would also not hear about is the fact that the U.S. Dollar is losing its reserve status, and irregardless of this fact the Federal Reserve is printing epic sums of currency causing a critical imbalance in supply and demand for U.S. Dollars. You would also not hear, despite the rising stock markets at this time, that GDP is falling with no recovery in sight as GDP is a measure of the employed and resulting corporate profits.

Before we really get going, in order to understand how things work in this super game we are going to have to learn a little bit more about ourselves, what drives us, what influences our thoughts and actions, and how these mechanisms will determine who will come out of this thing we are all going to witness unscathed, much the better, or not at all. Regardless of what you may believe at this moment your very behavior, in fact in many ways the person you are right now has been "caused to happen." For example, let's say you were born in a part of the world with little or no exposure to a television, advertisements, or education. Or perhaps reared in a nomadic African tribe, or brought up by wolves. Do you think you would be the same person you are now? Dress the same? Act the same, or think the same thoughts?

The social structure we live in and adapt to as a whole decides who and what you are to a great extent. Here in the United States we have information overload to the nth degree, and not all of this information is there to help you to succeed, in fact a great deal of the information is distributed with the intent to cause you to fail. Let me ask you, how is it that throughout history certain individuals were able to persuade throngs of people to follow them? To do things they knew in their hearts was morally wrong? What causes us to act in a specific manner or make us go this way when we just could have easily gone the other?

In order to understand what causes us to do "this instead of that" we are going to need answers to these questions, and we will do just that throughout this book. The decisions we make with regard to what we purchase, how we invest, how we raise our families, etc. are heavily influenced by "invisible factors." There are also "ominous factors," things which through the disbursement of misinformation cause a change in perception and as such influence the decisions we make to the benefit of others. As an example of how some of these "factors" work, let me speak briefly about my first book. That book included a new basic strategy system which took into account the evolution of the game of blackjack. The most basic changes was the moving from one deck used in play, to multiple decks shuffled together. I also took into consideration how the rules for the game had also changed over time. What I would consider to be an "invisible factor" with regard to this game is this: as the deck's of cards are played out during the game, each card taken out of play changes the overall composition of the deck, therefore a "perfect strategy" would have to take this into account. Being that most of the cards in blackjack have a value of 10, *and this is especially true for the multiple deck games,* as the game progresses it is much more beneficial for the player to "hit" on hands that he would never consider hitting on in a single deck game. And it worked! I consider this an "invisible factor" simply because the average player would not think about the composition of the deck changing as the game is played out.

The invisible factors involved in either a blackjack game, or anything else weigh heavily on who wins and who loses. This is why being educated with regard to any undertaking is critical, as these "invisible factors" can and will eat you alive. The "ominous factors" involved with regard to my effective system of blackjack was the misinformation which I believe was being put out by the casinos regarding my strategy. My system worked hands down and I made a small fortune using it at the time, and so did many of my readers, but then something very interesting happened. I started getting letters and emails from people who had been using my system saying it was becoming very hard for them to find games meeting the criteria I describe in my book. In direct response to my new blackjack strategy the casinos changed the rules for the game! Today it is very difficult to find a game in which a "blackjack" pays 3:2; most games since the publication of my strategy now pay just 6:5 for a "blackjack." Not only did my strategy cause the casinos to make this one major change, it also forced them to alter the rules regarding splitting cards and what hands could be doubled down on. Admittedly the changes instituted by the casinos effectively killed the game. I suppose in some ways it could be said that my blackjack book was a milestone book in that only one time before in gaming history were the rules for a modern casino game changed because of a new strategy for the game of blackjack. Today the game of blackjack is now unbeatable over the long run no matter what system you may choose to use. The fact that the game was beatable at one time is what drew many people to the game.

My first book is out of print now and it originally sold for around 12 bucks. If you were to go on Amazon right now and try to get one an unread copy is going for somewhere around a hundred bucks! Wow, who knew? Ironically I don't even have a copy for myself anymore as I gave them all away.

Be aware, there is another way which the "ominous factors" can work against you. The first one I spoke about was by the proliferation of misinformation, and the second is by withholding information. Each of these are equally deceptive.

The invisible factors come about simply by not being aware, the ominous factors are meant to deliberately mislead whether by inclusion of the wrong information or excluding the right information. By having an understanding of the "invisible" factors, it is exceedingly difficult to be deceived by the "ominous" factors which brings us full circle. Educate yourself about whatever you choose to do or choose not to do, and you will always be the better for it.

Take No Prisoners

This economic super game is as close to a winner takes all that I have ever come to know, and in order to play this mega game out to conclusion you have to understand the parameters. In fact this economic/political game is being played with stakes so high it has the potential to, *and will,* wipe out the lives in the literal sense of most of the world's population and we are witnessing the beginnings of that right now. The rules? Yes this game has rules just like the game blackjack does, and these rules are not the same for everyone.

It's Not Just About Wall Street

I empathize with the Occupy Wall Street Movement however, their efforts in my opinion are somewhat misdirected. It seems that a lot of their discontent is over there being such a great gap between those that have, and those that have a lot less. The problem I have with this thought process is this: an almost total misunderstanding of how it got this way, and it got that way not just by Wall Street, but by Main Street. It was the perception that the party would never end of those on Main Street which drove the massive real estate/housing bubble, and it was the popping of the housing bubble which is the root cause for a great deal of today's economic woes in the U.S. In fact more than likely it was the parents of those involved in OWS who helped drive the stock market and the real estate markets to unsustainable levels leading to their collapse. Oh you would never, ever, hear a policymaker say such a thing, but it is the plain, hard, cold, truth.

What OWS should be concerned about is not where we have been, but where we are going regarding the Federal Reserve's unrelenting attack on the American people as a whole by continuing to destroy the value of the dollar and crushing savers offering then negative returns on their interest earning accounts. Earlier I elaborated on how the general public tends to take advantage of an opportunity too late, well here, even if OWS continues to grow it is way too late. The plain truth is we have already hit a critical mass with regard to the financial/economic meltdown hurling our way. What those in the OWS movement should be doing is preparing for what is to come. What is important for people to realize is that the investment banks and those who's anger is being directed at by OWS could not possibly care less if we are in either an economic boom or a depression headed for a collapse. All they are concerned with is how to capitalize on the situation. We as individuals are like insects to them and honestly you should be OK with that and I will tell you why. All of this presents us, you and me, with unprecedented opportunity. For those on the inside this is like the goose which lays the golden eggs. An opportunity like this is a once in a lifetime thing so don't be upset, you are learning how to make it all work for you here with this book. I will tell you something else, the investment banks and major corporations which are two parts of the same thing, along with policymakers as well, do not care where the economy as a whole is going. They are for the most part, *as there are a few policymakers who do care*, a group which I like to call collectively the "politicocorporatists."

The politicocorporatists represent the merger between the policymakers and the corporate powers. In using the term corporate powers again, I am encompassing the major corporations and the investment banks. The people who are responsible for the operations of these companies have one thing in mind, and that is their own interests and that of their families and why? Because they are well aware that the endgame is at hand and unless you are an insider within that said company, meaning a member of the board or a major shareholder, your interests simply do not matter.

Today on a global level we are witnessing a phenomenon, a truly epic unfolding of events the likes of which have never been seen or witnessed before in human history. However most people have no idea what is happening or how these events are going to affect them. I am not just talking about your average Joe here. I am talking about highly educated people, money managers, and investors. There are so many factors at play from deliberate market manipulation to outright lies about some kind of economic recovery that by far the vast majority of the American people simply have no clue as to what is going to befall them, and even less of an idea of how to capitalize from it. For most people it is just like noise, hard to interpret, difficult to understand, and this is a product of how they are deliberately being made to feel. Today it is very difficult for the average person to simply carry out a typical day. We get up early, get dressed, and go to work where we have to deal with 8+ hours of stress, then come home exhausted, go to sleep, and repeat the same thing day after day year after year. Yes it is extremely difficult to do all these things while at the same time paying attention to this thing, or that thing.

What ends up happening is peoples' brains stops functioning normally and falls into a rhythm, or pattern, and blocks out almost everything else, it is a self preservation defense mechanism. In my professional medical opinion the typical pattern type incredibly stressful lifestyle that the vast majority of us are forced to live is the leading cause for disease bar none. When I was in school studying medicine I had to write a paper outlining the effects of stress on the body's immune system and the results are conclusive. When the body undergoes stress the adrenal cortex releases cortisol which is a natural steroid, when released in the body it causes several things to happen, one of which is a suppression of the body's immune system. The suppression of the body's immune system leaves the body open to attack by bacteria, viruses, fungi, and all manner or microorganism causing various diseases. Prolonged exposure to stress, the kind you would expect as a by product of living a stressful/average lifestyle and thus having excess corticosteroid within the body not only leads to increased risk of infections caused by microbes, but stroke, heart attack, hypertension, cancer, obesity, mental disorders, and premature death. All of this is documented medical fact.

In the medical science of psychology there is a condition known as "a normalcy bias." A normalcy bias can cause a rational person to reject the blatantly obvious. The fear of change, even if that change could save that persons life is dismissed by the individual or even in some cases masses of people who may be drawn into a situation which seems impossible or farfetched. Those who are affected with a normalcy bias tend to say things like, "Something like that has never happened here before, so I just don't believe it will ever happen." You can easily foresee the possible ramifications of this type of thought process.

I do not wish to downplay the severity of the crisis which is unfolding, apocalyptic would be a better word to describe what I and many others with a clear understanding of how this game is going to play out foresee occurring.

The biggest mistake which any person can make is to underestimate the severity of a given situation. Many battles and total wars have been lost because of underestimation. Underestimating has caused many a nation to collapse, corporations to lose market share, business to fail, investments to suffer, and people to die, among other things as well. It is always better to over prepare, because being unprepared when a crisis hits almost always leads to utter failure.

Sun Tzu the Art of War tells us that its is always better to have the high ground, and to be first on the field of battle.

Section 1

We Are Not All Drinking The Same Kool-Aid

The first thing to be absolutely sure of is this: the rules for this game are not standardized, they are vastly different favoring some over others. In gaming terms the deck is stacked against you. Who are the main players of this game? Simple: the White House and Wall Street, the politicocorporatists. To narrow this down even further we can safely say the policymakers in Washington and the investment banks. These two entities in every sense are in bed together, in fact today they can be regarded as one and the same. They are equal participants in a "super" game in which there can be only one conclusion. There is in fact one more major player in this game however for now let's just focus on these two. I will tell you who the third prime player is later on in section 2.

With a show of hands, how many of you believe that with regard to trading stock XYZ you are privy to the same information say the CEO of Goldman Sachs is? Or on issues of policy's or upcoming laws and regulations you have the same knowledge as a Congressman? Or if you decide to trade commodities, you are made aware before time of an upcoming margin change requirement? It goes on and on and on and here is where is gets even better, not only do those on the inside act upon information that you and I are not privy to and get handsomely rewarded financially, they are not prosecuted. In fact if you are a member of Congress it's actually legal for you to act on non-public information.

Below is an excerpt which was taken from the Wall Street Journal, (WSJ) 11-16-11.

To the extent our legislators are trading on their own unique political knowledge, at least they are thinking about the impact of their policies on productive businesses. To the extent they make a quick profit, at least they are paying the top personal tax rate, so helping to finance the spending they inflict on the rest of us. After all, the real scandal isn't what they do with their own money, but what they do with ours.

The Free Market Is Dead

OK. So we are now beginning to understand that the game is rigged, now what? Well, what else do we know? We absolutely know the free market is dead and therefore a whole new set of rules exist. From the time the government decided to institute the Troubled Asset Relief Program, (TARP), under then president Bush the free market was dead. In a free market those who have made bad bets are supposed to fail, it is the most basic principal in a free capitalistic society. No where in the constitution of the United States is there such a provision where the public is supposed to bail out failing corporations and or individuals for that matter. Now you and I, the public, own all of the bad bets placed by irresponsible financial institutions across the board. Assets which are still depreciating in value and who's price tag has been added to the National Debt. The writers of the constitution warned explicitly against such measures.

Not only did the free market essentially die, a whole new form of government was instituted. We now have a corporate state controlled by the government, aka the policymakers and the investment banks and as such the politicocorporatists were created. I will go one step further. The terrorist attacks of September 11, 2001 presented an unprecedented opportunity to those who were seeking to usurp the government of the United States. They succeeded. So yes the rules have changed. Not only have the rules been altered greatly skewing the odds in the favor of the well informed, but the playing field itself has also changed dramatically.

In the equity markets of today fifty percent of market action is High Frequency Trading, and HFT adds massive liquidity to the markets. Well financed players can and do take advantage of this mode, (HFT), of trading by deliberately manipulating the price of equities through collusion. It is very difficult for market oversight to recognize collusion with HFT because of 2 factors. The first is the modality of HFT itself it is very complex and mostly run by computer programs, and the second is High Frequency trades themselves take advantage of extremely brief moments of change in an asset's price and some of these changes are deliberately caused to happen.

Manipulating market prices of just about anything is done quite simply and frequently. Central banks manipulate asset prices all the time, one of the many ways in which they do it is with something called Gold Swaps. Using gold swaps, world central banks can pass or "swap," large amounts of gold for foreign currency or other assets either between each other or foreign governments. The effect of these transactions is simple, market manipulation in either the price of gold, currency exchange rates, etc. These "swaps" are fostered through what is known as the BIS which is an abbreviation for Bank for Internal Settlements. The BIS is the world's central banks, bank. In 1944 the Czech Republic accused the BIS of laundering gold which was stolen by the Nazi's during their blitz through Europe. The BIS states that it, along with the world's central banks, maintain international financial stability. I call it "influencing the world markets for the benefit the central bankers." The BIS is self governed, is under no countries jurisdiction, and does not answer to anyone. The BIS along with the world's central banks can manipulate and twist the world markets however they please at any time they want.

Currency values are highly manipulated as well, For example: the Chinese buy American dollars in order to manipulate exchange rates so they can keep the value of the dollar high in relation to the Yuan. This is done to assure that Chinese exports are kept "cheap." In fact the Chinese hold the largest reserves of foreign currency in the world for this very reason, to manipulate currency rates. The Chinese know how to play the game, in fact they make the rules when it comes to currency trading.

Basic economics tells us that an asset's price is driven by supply and demand. While supply and demand drivers are responsible to a certain degree with regard to the market price of an item, the main price driver of a given entity is psychological, driven by fear and greed. More on this later on but for now it is important to keep in mind that the price of any trade-able item can and is easily manipulated to illicit a specific response. In fact today so much market activity is manipulated in some way it is hard to discern reality from fantasy.

Running a close second to China with regard to market manipulation is The Federal Reserve. However, a more likely scenario is they are both equally guilty of tremendous amounts of market manipulation spanning the gamut. With regard to the rhetoric coming from the politicocorporatists and parroted by the mass media let's start with this: there is no real market/economic recovery. None, zero, zilch. In fact there will not be any real recovery until the overall markets are permitted to correct, or more precisely allowed to do their sole job. The single job of the equities markets is to determine fair market value, that's it, but this prime aspect of the markets has subsequently been stripped away and what we now have is enormous manipulation across the board. The massive manipulation in the markets must be understood for what it actually is, a last ditch effort by the politicocorporatists to push off the inevitable bursting of the bond and dollar bubbles. This is an event which will foster the conclusion of the greatest wealth transfer scheme the world has ever seen and something which has in fact been underway for quite some time. Consider this, the crash of 2008 took 38% of the wealth away from the aggregate American public, and this next crash will make 2008 look like a walk in the park.

The Fed has been manipulating the U.S. markets extensively since the housing price correction/stock market correction began, however due to direct intervention/manipulation the correction was not allowed to play out to conclusion. The politicocorporatists started it all with the "too big to fails." Please allow me elaborate on the most powerful and effective manipulation method known to and by man, it's called **fear**. If you can cause people to have fear you can control and manipulate their behavior. It is very simple and totally effective. Every day we are bombarded with adds, television commercials, all manner of devices which attempt to cause us to favor this product over that, or do this and not that, etc, etc. Governments take this to the extreme and instill fear into the mass public to cause their desired effect.

To further illustrate how the institution of fear is utilized by government upon its people here is a quote I would like you to read and consider:

"Naturally, the common people don't want war; neither in Russia nor in England nor in America, nor for that matter in Germany. That is understood. But, after all, it is the leaders of the country who determine the policy and it is always a simple matter to drag the people along, whether it is a democracy or a fascist dictatorship or a Parliament or a Communist dictatorship."

That quote was from Herman Goring who knew a little about how governments deliberately manipulate human behavior. Herman Goring was a leading member of the Nazi party, and was Commander in Chief of the German air force during World War II. He was second in command only to Adolf Hitler himself.

Carter G. Woodson, who was an American historian, educator, and author, had this to say:

"If you can control a man's thinking you do not have to worry about his action. When you determine what a man shall think you do not have to concern yourself about what he will do."

It is also important to keep in mind that having control of the information dispersed to the masses through media outlets is of critical importance. Keeping people distracted through the use of the mass media is very decisive tool. Up until the last days of WWII the German people believed that they were winning the war because that is what the media was telling them.

Simple economics would also have us believe that there are cycles in all economies, meaning that is there are up cycles followed by down cycles and so on. What is occurring now in America is not anywhere near or like a simple economic down cycle. If we were in a simple downward economic cycle as they would have us believe, the Fed. would not be trying so desperately to manipulate the overall market. The truth is the Fed. is in panic mode and the same is true for all the world's central banks.

Let's Talk More About There Being No Real Recovery

Prior to the Fed's quantitative easing (QE1) also known as currency printed out of thin air (1.7 trillion dollars), the stock market had corrected nearly 50 percent and housing was in also in a downward spiral. Then like magic the Fed. initiated QE and poof! The market began to rebound and the falling housing prices slowed, then QE ended. What happened next? The equity markets began to fall and housing again began to speed their downward trajectory. No worries, here comes QE2 (another 1.7 trillion dollars) and again poof! The overall markets improved. Then when QE2 ended markets again began to falter and the Fed. initiated operation twist. Operation twist and now twist 2, are simply ridiculous terms used to describe bond swaps. What the Fed. is doing is swapping out short term bonds for long term bonds and is also using nearly another 300 billion dollars which were "left over" from QE2 to also purchase more long term bonds. With all this the Fed. has been successful in keeping interest rates at historic and artificial lows and greatly increasing the currency in circulation, and thus debasing the currency.

In a statement made by Fed. Chairman Ben Bernanke during one of his meetings, he declared "The Fed. will keep interest rates low through 2013." But wait, QE2 was supposed to have ended. Without overtly admitting it, the Fed. just initiated QE3. Understand, the Fed. can't just go ahead and "say" we are continuing to keep interest rates low, it has to actually get into the market and make it happen. In this case the Fed. is continuing to buy long term bonds with currency printed out of thin air and will continue to do so until at least 2013. All this market manipulation by the Fed. gives the illusion of some type of economic recovery, but it is simply not there. Housing has not recovered, in fact it will continue to fall, and unemployment despite all the government's efforts continues to be high. The stock market loves all this cheap currency being printed by the Fed. rebounding from a low of around 6,500 because it allows speculation in the market, but as soon as the fruit punch is taken away it too will drop. The reasons why both the real estate market and the stock market have to resume their downward trajectory are two fold. First: market forces were and are continuing to be artificially manipulated to cause them to rebound. Second: the fundamental reasons why they were falling still exist. In a healthy economy yes, market cycles do exist, but today we have anything but a healthy economy that is just in a normal economic downturn. All the parameters have changed dramatically, and will continue to do so. It must be understood that the main drivers of our economy are gone and will not return for decades if ever. The economy of the United States is driven by consumer spending, in fact seventy percent of it. During the housing boom, right up until its inevitable collapse our economy and our markets were the envy of the world. It was simple greed which drove this economic engine at an unsustainable rate. The meteoric rise in the price of housing and other real estate asset's in the United States was driven by the factor of greed fueled by cheap available cash. The rise in real estate asset's was disproportionate with incomes and economic growth, and any liability which continues to rise in this manner is in a bubble, and all economic bubbles pop. There are no exceptions.

During this time of prosperity people spent cash on everything in excess. Unemployment was low and people were creating wealth. Even so, many people used their appreciating real estate asset's as banks drawing on its increasing value which seemed like it would never end. Banks were giving out mortgages to everyone and anyone like candy. Many of these people were sub-prime but the banks didn't care and neither did the people buying these homes. Many of the people had no interest in keeping the homes and simply wanted to flip the home and turn a quick profit. So the terms of these loans didn't matter either. No one, obviously not even the people making these loans ever thought the party would end. Rising real estate values were here to stay! Just didn't turn out that way. Therefore since the popping of the housing bubble, all the rules have changed. With the popping of the housing bubble poof! There goes the main driver of consumer spending. The rise of the housing bubble which was the main driver of economic growth since the 1980's is gone. The epic rise of real estate values along with the massive consumer spending driven by that rise had paved the way for businesses to thrive and jobs to be created. All of that is finished, totally played out. Therefore without that main driver of economic growth whatever the Fed. tries to do or grandstanding by President Obama nothing can bring it back. The jobs which were lost during the deflating of the housing bubble are not coming back. The drivers of a healthy economy simply in a downturn do not exist anymore, instead what we have is a perfect storm which has not even come close to its full devastating power yet.

We are in for far more that a prolonged "depression," we are just about staring into a financial abyss. However, it is at times like this that fortunes will be made for some, that is if you know how to play the game. Much of the blame for the current economic crisis has been placed upon the "sub-prime" borrower but in reality this is not the case. The bursting of the housing bubble was actually caused by a scheme which was dreamed up and instituted by two of the world's biggest banks (now defunct) Bear Stearns and Lehman Bros.

Both Bear Stearns and Lehman Brothers took on loans which they knew were bad involving mortgage backed securities, packaged them up, and sold them off to unknowing investors and other banks. The debt involved in these fraudulent deals became highly leveraged via derivative trades and epic sums were lost as the reality that these supposed good loans (which were rated AAA) were actually bad. This scam was a major contributory factor in the crash of 2008 in which the aggregate American people lost nearly 40% of their net worth. Still, where are the arrests? Status post the crash of 2008 other financial institutions like Barclay's, (and 16 other major banks involved in interest rate rigging LIBOR), as well as MF Global, JP Morgan Chase, HSBC, Capital One, and Bank of America have all been involved in criminal activity spanning the gamut up to and including money laundering for drug cartels, *and no arrests have been made to date.*

Some people would argue that there has been a rise in gross domestic product (which is now subsequently falling) since the end of the great recession. I would say really? And here is why: never before in the history of the United States has there been such enormous government spending during a "downward economic cycle," which adds to GDP. If you were to calculate out the immense spending the government has done attempting to pump up our dying economy which would include cash printed out of thin air by the Fed. to purchase long term bonds, (by the way so far the Fed. has increased the currency supply over three hundred percent and counting since 2008), you would get negative GDP, no growth, in fact you would have contraction.

This is a chart of what a 300% increase in the currency supply looks like:

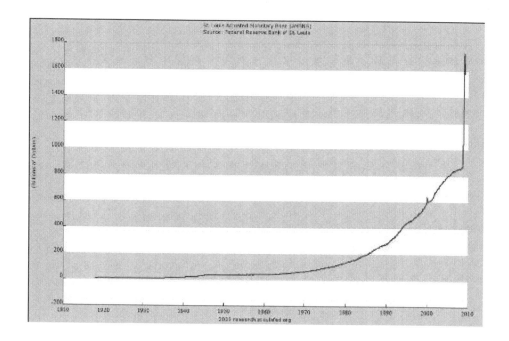

What you see in the chart about is unprecedented and very dangerous. The epic increase in the money supply is causing a greater and greater imbalance in the supply and demand for dollars. This issue is a major contributing factor in the massive inflation which we will have in the future.

The Bigger They Are The Harder They Fall

Having an understanding of the game rules makes it easy to play and win. They say a picture is worth a thousand words so let's look at some charts.

Take a look at this chart.

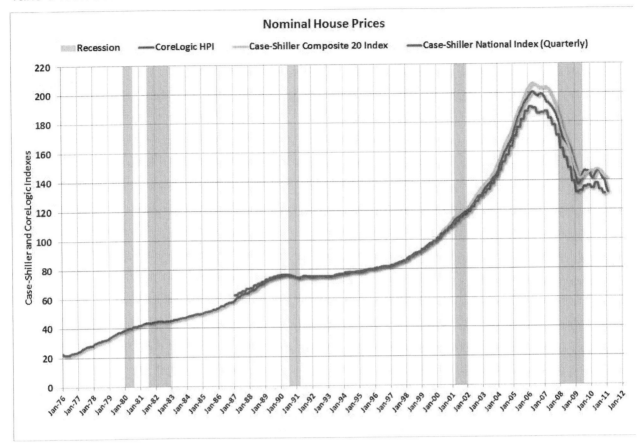

This chart above demonstrates a clear bubble pattern, in this case the housing bubble. What can also be gleaned from this chart is clearly real estate prices have more to fall, (although since the time of this writing housing seems to be stabilizing). Right now housing prices seem to have slowed and in some parts of the country have even begun to rise. However, this is solely due to intervention from the Fed. and not due to any positive fundamentals within the real estate market. If anything the fundamentals within the real estate market are still deteriorating, and much of that is due to the fact that the Fed. purchased trillions in toxic assets under TARP, assets which are now owned by the public.

The current Federal Reserve's economic policy's are not only destined to fail for many reasons which will be discussed throughout this book, but are actually making the long term problems much, much worse, devastatingly so actually.

Its All About Fair Market Value

It must be understood that all market forces seek one thing, and that is fair market value, that is their sole job if you will. All the collusion, market manipulation by the Fed., etc. etc. has to fail over time because the market forces are enormous, way bigger that any entity'(s) efforts to control it. At this point in time because of the continuing market manipulation by the Fed. the world's biggest bubble is being created, a super mega bubble. When this bubble pops, which is something we are starting to already see in Europe, every remaining economic bubble which still exists, not just only here in the United States but globally are going to tumble until they over-correct. It is unfortunate that government and non-government entities, (the Fed. and the other world central banks), believe that they can control the markets. Because of this people around the globe are going to suffer greatly. Let's look at this another way. The ratio of investors world wide to central bankers is about 10,000 to 1, yet the central bankers believe that they which represent a fraction of a percent know better how to "run the markets" better than the vast majority. They have refused to allow natural market dynamics/a free market to determine fair asset values, so they the vast minority solely because they have the power to do so keep acting upon the markets unnaturally and unilaterally. This repeated and direct market intervention is going to lead to financial devastation across the board sometime in the near future and here is why: before market dynamics force themselves into correction, the central banks of the world are going to continue to pump up the markets with the printing of massive amounts of fiat currency. This type of intervention is going to compound the problem exponentially. In fact they are going to try and come up with and impose any and every conceivable scheme ever devised in trying to push off the popping of this mega bubble, but when the eventual forced market correction occurs at that point the ramifications are going to shake the world.

Understand, the only way they can push off the inevitable collapse is to compound the root cause of the problem, excessive and massive debt. Its like trying to save a drowning man by throwing more water on him. Take a look at the chart of the DOW below.

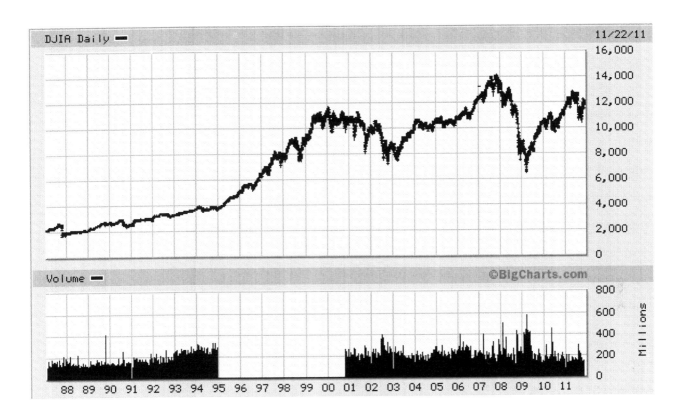

If you look at this chart and the previous chart of the housing index it is clear that the housing boom fueled the subsequent stock market boom. There is also a clear lag. The housing boom really got going in the 1980's and this fueled consumer spending, created jobs, allowed businesses to grow, and then in the early 1990's caused the spike in the equity markets. At the very moment real estate prices began to fall the equity markets followed suit, there was no lag time. This should demonstrate to you how important the relationship is between real estate and the equity market, and it should also demonstrate to you why the Federal Reserve is so "Hell Bent" on trying to pump up real estate values and not allowing them to correct to their fair market value.

33

The Fed. believes that by artificially stimulating businesses this will create jobs, while this policy may create some jobs in the short run as soon as the fruit punch is taken away poof! There goes those artificially created jobs. In order for there to be a sustained and "real" economic recovery substantial economic drivers need to be created. The Fed's stimulus does not create economic drivers, it only creates an artificial environment across the board... And, more debt.

The Greatest Ponzi Scheme Ever Sold

Let us define a Ponzi scheme. A **Ponzi scheme** is a fallacious investment activity which pays returns to its investors with their own currency or the cash paid into the scheme by subsequent investors. This scheme was made famous by Charles Ponzi who defrauded investors in this manner in the 1920's. Below is a mug shot of Charles Ponzi.

In what is the definition of a Ponzi scheme, the Federal Reserve truly runs the biggest of them all. Think about this. The Federal Reserve prints cash out of thin air, it is not backed by any hard asset, and then disperses this currency. Once this currency leaves the Federal Reserve it begins to acquire interest, interest which is paid back to the Federal Reserve with even more currency printed out of thin air. The Federal Reserve can then pay its shareholders profits in this manner and acquire hard assets like gold. It really is the greatest Ponzi scheme in human history.

Section 2
An Economy On Life Support

The major players are surely aware of how this game is going to play out, make no mistake about that. Who are the major players again? Yes, the policymakers and the investment banks but we shall call them the politicocorporatists. Let's explore the concept of the corporate elites being one and the same as the policymakers for a moment. Below I have included a list of several prior Goldman Sachs executives who currently or recently hold/held high positions in the U.S. government:

Dianna Farrell: *Obama Administration: Deputy Director, National Economic Council. Former Goldman Sachs Title: Financial Analyst.*

Stephen Friedman: *Obama Administration: Chairman, President's Foreign Intelligence Advisory Board. Former Goldman Sachs Title: Board Member (Chairman, 1990- 94; Director, 2005-).*

Gary Gensler: *Obama Administration: Commissioner, Commodity Futures Trading Commission. Former Goldman Sachs Title: Partner and Co-head of Finance.*

Robert Hormats: *Obama Administration: Undersecretary for Economic, Energy and Agricultural Affairs, State Department. Former Goldman Sachs Title: Vice Chairman, Goldman Sachs Group.*

Philip Murphy: *Obama Administration: Ambassador to Germany. Former Goldman Sachs Title: Head of Goldman Sachs, Frankfurt.*

Mark Patterson: Obama Administration: Chief of Staff to Treasury Secretary, Timothy Geitner. Former Goldman Sachs Title: Lobbyist 2005-2008; Vice President for Government Relations.

John Thain: Obama Administration: Advisor to Treasury Secretary, Timothy Geitner. Former Goldman Sachs Title: President and Chief Operating Officer (1999-2003).

Henry Paulson: Bush II Administration: Secretary, Treasury 2006 - 2009. Former Goldman Sachs Title: Chairman and CEO (1998-2006).

Neel Kashkari: Bush II Administration: Assistant Secretary for Financial Stability, Treasury (2008 – 2009). Former Goldman Sachs Title: Vice President, San Francisco; led Information Technology Security Investment Banking Practice.

Reuben Jeffery: Bush II Administration: Undersecretary for Economic, Energy and Agricultural Affairs, State Department (2007 –2009). Former Goldman Sachs Title: Managing Partner Paris until 2002 Security Investment Banking Practice.

Robert Steel: Bush II Administration: Under Secretary for Domestic Finance, Treasury, (2006 – 2008). Former Goldman Sachs Title: Vice Chairman – 2004.

Steve Shafran: Bush II Administration: Advisor on setting up TARP to Treasury Secretary, Henry Paulson 2008. Former Goldman Sachs Title: Private Equity Business in Asia until 2000.

Edward C. Forst: Bush II Administration: Advisor on setting up TARP to Treasury Secretary, Henry Paulson 2008. Former Goldman Sachs Title: Co-head of Goldman's Investment Management Business.

Dan Jester: Bush II Administration: Advisor on setting up TARP to Treasury Secretary, Henry Paulson 2008. Former Goldman Sachs Title: Deputy CFO.

Kendrick R. Wilson III: Bush II Administration: Advisor on setting up TARP to Treasury Secretary, Henry Paulson 2008. Former Goldman Sachs Title: Chairman of Goldman's Financial Institutions Groups.

Joshua Bolten: Bush II Administration: White House Chief of Staff (2006 – 2009). Former Goldman Sachs Title: Executive Director, Legal & Government Affairs (1994-99).

Gary Gensler: Bush II Administration: Undersecretary, Treasury (1999-2001) and Assistant Secretary, Treasury (1997-1999). Former Goldman Sachs Title: Partner and Co-head of Finance.

Robert Rubin: Bush II Administration: Secretary, Treasury 1995-1999. Former Goldman Sachs Title: Vice Chairman (1987-90).

Robert Zoellick: Bush II Administration: United States Trade Representative (2001-2005), Deputy Secretary of State (2005-2006), World Bank President (2007). Former Goldman Sachs Title: Vice Chairman, International (2006-07).

William C Dudley: NY Federal Reserve: Current President/CEO. Former Goldman Sachs Title: Partner and Managing Director – 2007.

So What Is Really Going On Here?

Clearly Wall Street insiders are deeply embedded and involved in establishing the rules of this economic super game. In fact with regard to the TARP program: then treasury secretary Henry Paulson under Bush got Congress to approve a seven hundred billion dollar payout using U.S. tax payer dollars for his Wall Street buddies, (more on this later), and how did he do it? He did it by telling Congress and the American people if they decided not to do it America would collapse financially and immediately. Paulson used the oldest and most effective trick in the book to get TARP passed, fear. Would America have collapsed financially without the TARP program? Absolutely not. Well what would have happened? The bad investments made by the investment banks would have been written off as losses, or partial losses, bonuses for the executives of these corporations would have been a bit less although still in the multiple seven figure range. But then perhaps some fundamental changes to the way investment banks take unnecessary risks would have been implemented, and better business models would have emerged. Instead no changes were made, the public, you and me, now own tens of billions in toxic assets including bad mortgages which continue to deteriorate and will do so for the foreseeable future. If Congress had actually put the American people first and did not approve TARP yes, there would have been some temporary financial pain and economic slowing which would have in turn put pressure on Congressional leaders who would be facing re-election. However the policymakers could not allow their political contributors to suffer one iota of pain, so they gave it to you instead. The major problem is this: because of the relationship between the policymakers and the investment banks, the commons which are you and me are being prepared for the slaughter yet to come. Understand this and I will elaborate more on this later on. A financial wrecking ball is aimed straight at your head, it is unstoppable and it is approaching fast but don't worry, I am going to teach you how not only how to remove the target from the middle of your forehead, but also how you are going to capitalize on this upcoming event big time!

With the popping of the housing bubble and the refusal of the politicocorporatists to allow natural market dynamics to take effect and correct in a normal way, what is being created is a financial monster. In a free market natural forces drive and direct asset prices, therefore over valued asset's correct downward and under priced asset's correct upward. What we have now is an equity market being pumped up by cheap currency and a housing market not being allowed to normalize. We also have an overall fake economic recovery being artificially suspended for the same reasons. Once the forces which are being used by the Fed. in collusion with the investment banks are stopped either by themselves, or involuntary pushed upon them by the massive natural market dynamics which eventually will prevail it's party over. It is important to understand that natural market forces are enormous, and all this pumping up cannot be sustained by any means. At some point market dynamics will prevail and force a major corrective move. Since 2008 the Fed. has increased the currency supply 300% as I had mentioned earlier. Just think about that for another moment. The Federal Reserve in order to slow the drop of real estate values and to pump up the equity markets has had to increase the currency supply by three hundred percent. To get another visual on this, take a look again at this chart below.

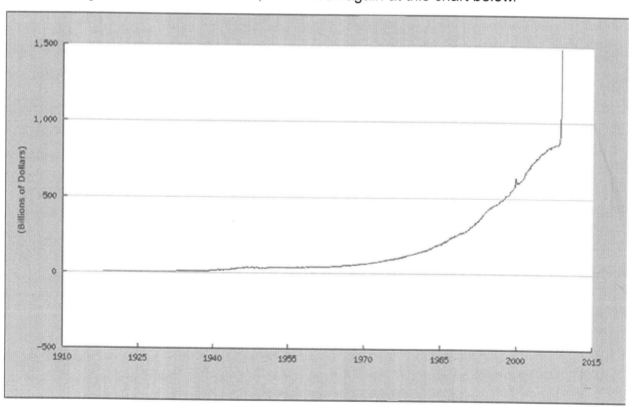

The chart on the previous page visually demonstrates the incredible parabolic move the monetary base has undergone since 2008 from the Fed. literally printing currency. Does this pattern look familiar to you? It is a classic bubble pattern and an economic bubble cannot be sustained. Look at the steady sloping increase in the monetary base from 1985, this was a natural increase in the cash supply due to a booming economy. Now observe the parabolic move caused by the Fed's currency printing. This is anything but natural or caused by a booming economy, or anything for that matter which may be seen in a typical economic slowdown during a healthy economy. It is unprecedented. So from the information in the chart it is clear that the Fed. has the printing presses fired up and running on mega overdrive. So what's the problem some people have asked me? The main problem is this: each dollar magically added to the monetary base by the Federal Reserve devalues each dollar already in circulation. That means that not in essence but in reality each day Ben Bernanke runs his printing press you are getting poorer. In fact ever since Ben pushed the panic button and cranked up his printing presses in 2008 your dollar has lost 15 percent of its value. Lets look at this another way. Lets say you have ten grand stuffed under your mattress, that ten grand will buy you the equivalent of eighty five hundred dollars worth of the same goods in today's currency. Old Ben is attacking you directly and financially more and more each and every day by running his printing presses in hyper mode. The Federal Reserve's current policies of devaluing the dollar more and more by printing epic sums of cash out of thin air is robbing the American people, rich and poor alike, by taking away the purchasing power of our currency. However, there is a simple strategy that counters this move, and I will elaborate on this later on. Please keep in mind, and this goes back to Newton's physical laws-Whenever there is a move in the direction of anything or an "action" as Newton would put it, there is always a counter-action. This counter-action is simply something the average sheep like person has no idea about, "an invisible factor," so they just kind of move along like little sheep going to the slaughter. Let's look at the chart on the next page to get a visual on how the Federal Reserve is making you broke.

The chart which follows is the dollar index which measures the value of the U.S. Dollar in relation to a basket of other currencies which include the Euro (EUR), Yen (JPY), Pound (GBP),Canadian dollar (CAD), Krona (SEK), and Franc (CHF).

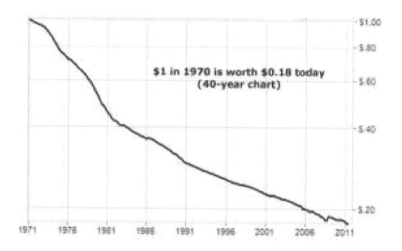

The Fed's currency printing policy is also punishing savers. Up until recently having a savings account or other investment vehicle that pays interest was a viable way to make your cash grow. Today with Ben keeping interests rates at historic and unnatural lows, these investments have negative returns, that is, the interest rates being paid are below the rate of inflation.

The Value Of Fiat

If you were to go on safari and just happened to come across a tribe of natives and say you ran out of supplies, how would you go about getting them from the tribal leaders? I suppose you could whip out your wallet and try to exchange your greenbacks for what you needed, however it would not get you anything. Unless of course the tribe needed some paper to keep a fire going I suppose, otherwise the value of your cash would be zero.

The Value Of Currency Is An Illusion

Today currency has no real value as demonstrated in the scenario above. Today we have a fiat currency system. Fiat is a Latin term for "so let it be." Here is how it works. The Federal Reserve (which is not a part of the government and is in fact run by private banks and other individuals) prints currency out of thin air, the same as if you were to make some counterfeit cash at home using your computer and printer, there is absolutely no difference. (Please do not do this, the Fed. is allowed to, you are not). This new cash is then distributed to the central banks of the individual states which then liquefy, meaning they then lend that new currency printed out of thin air to the commercial banks, and begin to charge interest on this currency created from nothing. So the Federal Reserve creates debt, which is all they create. The Fed prints cash from nothing, literally out of thin air, and then that cash "becomes real." This new cash is then owed back to the Federal Reserve in the form of debt plus any interest it may accrue. Wow, it must be great to be a central banker. Think about that scenario for a moment, the Federal Reserve creates debt owed to them plus interest from nothing. In my opinion this game played by the Fed. is the most notorious scam in the history of the world, and I have more to say about this gag later on. Before going off the gold standard the Federal Reserve was not able do this, that is it could not literally and simply just print cash out of thin air, *money was real*, and that is the sole reason why money was so much more valuable at that time, up until 1971.

Each dollar printed by the Federal Reserve during the gold standard had to be backed, by law as stated in the U.S. Constitution, by an equal amount of precious metal, and each coin minted also had to have a percentage of precious metal in it, namely silver. During the gold standard currency represented money, *gold and silver,* which was backing and subsequently stored in government stockpiles. Each and every penny, nickel, dime, quarter, etc. as well as every subsequent bill represented that actual money. Today the cash in your wallet, bank account, etc. has absolutely no real value.

The Federal Reserve bank prints cash from nothing, literally out of thin air, and creates debt in the form of these said monies which is owed back to them plus any accrued interest. And there my friend is the biggest scam which has ever been played upon the human race. But it gets much worse than that, read on. Consider this for a moment. If you were to go on eBay right now and look at say a 1964 dime, it would probably bid up to about $3.25, that's because a 1964 dime actually had value because it contains a small amount of real silver. Gold and silver have been methods of exchange for thousands of years, and are real wealth. During the gold standard currency represented real wealth (money) which is only gold and silver, and as such you could have taken your currency to any central bank and exchange that currency for money (gold and or silver) in the amount represented by that said currency. Let's go back to the 1964 dime for a moment. So a 1964 dime is worth about $3.25 in today's currency, what that means if we were still on a gold standard a gallon of gasoline would cost you just about a dime! Wow. Going off the gold standard, under Nixon, did not come without a hefty price. What we have seen since going off the gold standard is an over 90% drop in the value of currency and real money rise exponentially. What this has done is crush the consumer or holder of currency by destroying their purchasing power however, this rig has enriched the central bankers beyond anyone's imagination. Again they create debt owed to them plus interest from nothing. This is true for not just the Federal Reserve but all the world's central banks, which are also owned by the same people.

WARNING

You had better sit down before reading this next segment. Please do. If having a gold standard was so good, why was it abandoned in favor of a fiat currency system?
To finance the Vietnam War, that is the answer.

The U.S. government policymakers and the Military Industrial Complex needed to fund the Vietnam War, and with a gold standard in place they could not just print currency out of thin air like they can and do today. So the central bankers came up with the brilliant idea (brilliant for them), to abandon the gold standard and move to a fiat cash system. This way the government could have all the currency they want, *as now with a fiat monetary system the Fed. can simply print currency out of thin air,* which made the Military Industrial Complex very happy, and in turn made the central bankers immensely wealthy. It was a win, win situation for those involved in running the war, but a horrible despicable loss for those who were forced spill their blood and guts on the battle fields of Vietnam via the draft, and humanity as a whole. Why did we fight, and subsequently lose the Vietnam War anyway? Oh yes, to stop the spread of Communism. And how did the United States become involved in direct combat with the Vietcong? Well we the American sheep, I mean people, were told that the Vietcong attacked one of our warships, a destroyer called the USS Maddox in what was known as the Gulf of Tonkin incident, 1964. Now that is interesting, why would the Vietcong want to involve the United States in direct conflict? Why would they want to provoke the United States? In 1964 the Vietcong "navy" at that time consisted of antiquated WWII torpedo boats which were procured from France in the mid fifties. Lets set the scene here for a moment. So you are a Vietcong General already heavily involved in armed conflict with the South Vietnamese government. At a critical juncture like that, would you consider or even attempt to attack a modern American warship? And if you did go ahead for some twisted reason decide to send your men directly to their deaths and attack this modern ship of war, a U.S. destroyer, would you use antiquated torpedo boats? Knowing that if you did the war could escalate and directly involve the United States? I don't think you would. The American people were told that on August 2nd 1964 the Vietcong attacked the U.S.S. Maddox with 3, left over from WWII, French torpedo boats therefore America had to enter into direct military conflict with the Vietcong.

There are some who contend that the Gulf of Tonkin incident never even happened, and believe it was a story conjured up by the MIC to create a reason for the United States to get directly involved with the war. What ever the case may be, 58,209 American servicemen were killed along with multiple hundreds of thousands of Vietnamese combatants and non-combatants alike, and we also lost our gold standard.

WARNING IS STILL IN EFFECT

This brings me to the next and third major player in this economic super game. In section one I wrote about the politicocorporatists, that is the merger of the policymakers and the corporations and I also told you there was another major player involved. I am going to name them now, and I alluded to them in the previous pages. They are called the Military Industrial Complex. Who or what is the Military Industrial Complex? The Military Industrial Complex abbreviated (MIC) is also called the Military Industrial Congressional complex and refers to the policies and monetary relationships between policymakers, the armed forces, and the corporations which supports them. These relationships include political contributions, Congressional approval for defense spending, and other legislation which serves to further the interests of the MIC. Former President Eisenhower who before becoming President was a five star U.S. Army General during WWII filmed a warning to the American people about the MIC, I urge you to find it online and watch it.

So We Lose Our Gold Standard

The Constitution of the United States Article I: No state shall coin money; emit bills of credit; make anything but gold and silver coin a tender in payment of debt. Does that sound like the creating of fiat currency out of thin air to you? But is gets better than that! And truly the simplicity of it is pure wicked brilliance on the part of the policymakers, the central banks, major corporations especially those involved in creating weapons and other war sustaining goods and lastly the MIC.

As we are aware, the sole reason why we were taken off a gold standard by our policymakers in direct and dastardly collusion with the central bankers was to finance the Vietnam War, there is no question about that. We are also aware that at the same time we were taken off our gold standard, the petrodollar system was instituted in an arrangement between the central bankers, the MIC, and OPEC, (Organization of Petroleum Exporting Countries). This arrangement created a system in which an ever increasing demand for the Federal Reserve's fiat currency would exist and the dollar would then become the world's reserve currency. It should be obvious to you at this point that the United States involvement in the Vietnam War was used as a ploy in what in my opinion was the most wretched scheme ever devised, this strategy succeeded in vaulting the Federal Reserve's fiat currency system into a method of enslavement of the world by debt owed to directly to the Federal Reserve/central banks. I will also say: this scheme although devious beyond any words I could possibly choose to put down on paper, may have been the most brilliant folly played upon the human race.

Section 3
Fear And Greed

Market forces are only in part driven by supply and demand. Was it supply and demand which drove the cost of real estate to unrealistic levels? Absolutely not. How about if someone buys shares of stock in a company whose price to earnings, (PE) ratio, is 125:1? No to this one as well. So what does this tell us? Clearly supply and demand are not the only factors which drive the price of an item. The main driver of an asset is obviously not based upon fundamentals or a technical chart, it is psychological based upon perception. As real estate prices began to soar into the stratosphere going way beyond what incomes and economic fundamentals would dictate, very few people were able to appreciate that there was a major problem developing. All kinds of excuses were made as to why real estate prices were going literally through the roof. But the root cause was greed and everyone wanted a piece of the cheesecake. People see a particular asset rising fast, and as we all know people are always looking for that quick way to make cash, so what happens is greed begins to pervade and overtake rational thinking and like a tidal wave, a frenzy of asset accumulation begins. The problem with this behavior is frankly the general public lacks the knowledge needed to actually make these things work, so what happens is they end up get crushed, losing hefty sums on poor investments. The main reason for this is that way too many people tend to enter into a rising asset's price at the high end when the asset has already risen above realistic levels. Then people continue to hold onto this now toxic asset as the price corrects downward, leading to devastating losses. This scenario is exactly what happened to multitudes of people who bought real estate at the top of the housing bubble, hoping to cash in.

Even at this point in time the Federal Reserve is still holding tens of billions in toxic real estate assets and there are no buyers, this is one of the reasons why housing still has more to fall.

That wisdom along with the massive back log in foreclosed homes being held by these said banks, regardless of what action the Fed. is taking to try and support housing prices at this level, real estate prices still have further to slip. One more thing before I move on. If you are waiting for the value of your home to appreciate back up to or even near the top of the bubble, forget about it! Perhaps if you were to live 300 more years maybe, but not in yours or your children's lifetime. I am sorry to have to say this, but if you purchased your home at or near the top of the bubble you are now in possession of a toxic asset and my advice to you is get out of it anyway you can. Housing at a minimum, even from the point we are at today on a national level has to correct at least another 10 to 15% before it reaches fair market value.

Dot-Com

From the mid 1990's up until the year 2002 we experienced the information technology boom and bust, also known as the dot-com bubble. Take a look at this chart.

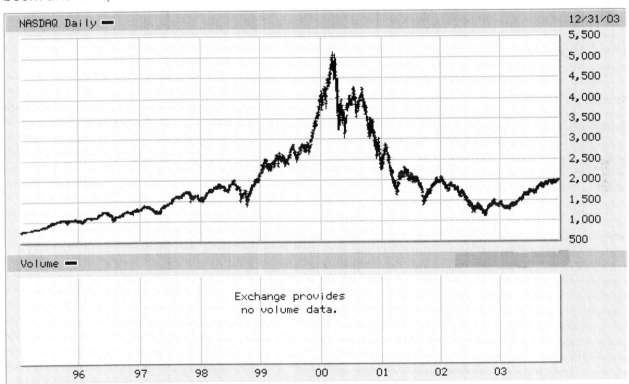

As you can see, the common theme in all these bubble charts is a meteoric rise followed by a crash or correction. Enormous amounts of cash were both made and lost in each of these occurrences. The smart "money" is made on both sides of the bubbles, long positions on the rise and short positions on the fall. The problem with any asset bubble is not that they form, it's that people generally get in way to late, somewhere near the top and then tend to stay long the positions on the way down. The reasons for this type of behavior is lack of knowledge of how the game is played. Now take a look at this chart.

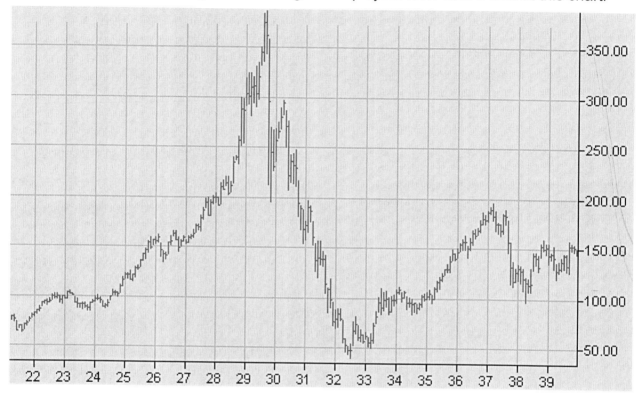

The chart above, *yes another clear bubble pattern*, is the stock market crash of 1929.

So What Caused The Crash of '29?

From 1925 to the third quarter of 1929 common stocks increased in value by 120 percent, that's it, period the end. There is no reason to open the history books and read possibly hundreds of pages or even perhaps several volumes of information on why the stock market crashed in 1929. For an asset, or any asset class for that matter to rise such a degree so fast is simply not sustainable or realistic. So it all comes down to this, consumer sentiment, the perception that the party would never end. Does any of this sound familiar to you? Its always the same story. Fundamentals, technical analysis, or any other measurable economic tool played no role. How could the value of any asset rise outside that which average incomes may be and the rate of economic growth to such a degree? It does not make sense, and as such a bubble was formed and it subsequently popped, period, the end. I put this chart here for another reason. I want to convey to you that these bubbles are in the grand scheme of things common occurrences and we are in the midst of the biggest bubble in human history right now. In any asset bubble the up side is caused by greed, and on the down side of the bubble you have fear. I want you to notice the over-correction in this particular chart, I circled it on this next chart.

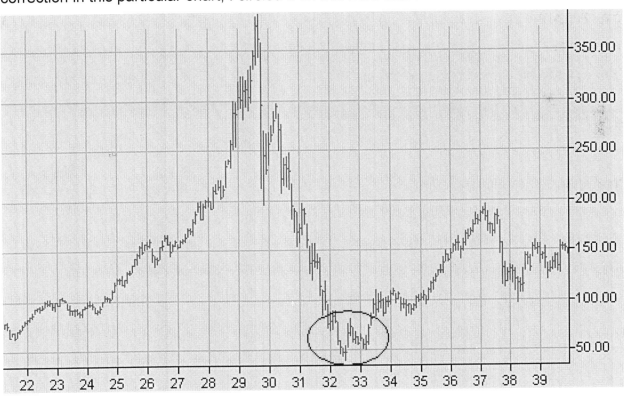

The reason a dropping asset tends to over-correct is because fear is actually stronger that greed. This is why it is so important to understand human behavior. Before I let the cat out of the bag, I will say this: the mother of all the bubbles ever created by man is already here, can you figure out what it is?

The Next Super Bubble

I mentioned that there was another bubble a few times already and I am going to elaborate on it at length in section 5. Taking advantage of this super bubble is why I wrote this book. ****I will tell you a secret, another super bubble is now in its very early stages right now, and that is something else we are going to capitalize on!**

So I hope that I have established for you that greed brought on by a misguided perception is the single predominant factor in why all these asset bubbles were created, and it is also what we insiders count on. Insiders like you are becoming, now simply sit and wait while all the sheep, *the uninformed fly by the seat of their pants type of people,* line up for the slaughter and then we give it to them good. It's not that these sheep like people types deserve it, they just either do not have the foresight, lack sufficient drive, cannot think outside the box, and a host of other things. My point is I wish more people would at least try to understand those things which have enormous potential to both help and hurt them and their families. I wish people would read more, educate themselves, but unfortunately most will not.

In any game there are winners and there are losers and that's the way it is. It is like poker, which is a game I play a lot of. We sit and lurk like hungry sharks just waiting for the "donkeys" as we call them to sit down at the table with us, and then we eat their lunch for them and we leave the table with their cash. Why do these donkeys lose their cash? We are not any smarter than they are, we just understand how the game is played to a higher degree because we study it. We are willing to put the required time in to learn the game, and the Politics Of Money is the biggest game of them all.

Let me say this, if you have gotten through the information I have presented thus far in this book and are beginning to grasp some of these concepts you are way ahead of the game already, and I am personally proud of you. There is a huge amount of information here.

Not only is it greed which drives the price of an asset way beyond with the fundamentals dictate, it is also greed that causes these same people to lose ridiculous amounts of cash. These people, just like the donks at the poker table are entering into a realm they should never have gotten into in the first place and why? Because their greed, or visions of grandeur get the better of them.

Fear

We have discussed in earlier sections of this book how fear is used as a tool to influence human behavior. It is also fear which is a driver of an asset's price, in this case downward pressure. What tends to happen when an asset price or the overall market falls rapidly it tends to over-correct That is the price falls below its fair market value and this is when a real buying opportunity occurs. Earlier on in section one I presented you with a chart of the U.S. housing price index. What I suspect would have happened if the Fed. had not stepped in and tried to pump the housing prices back up, (something that has no chance of working in the long run because the massive and powerful market forces will eventually prevail for reasons I discuss throughout this book), is housing would have continued to drop to the point of over-correction. This scenario is still going to occur and I will discuss more on this in section 4 .

More Greed

As outlined in the previous section, under President Nixon and the MIC along with the central banks we lost our gold standard. This move although brilliant for some, ensuring massive financial wealth and a virtual endless supply of "fake" currency to fight the Vietnam War as well as any other war the MIC wishes to force upon the American people, dealt a devastating blow to the common people.

As the value of the now fiat dollar began its long and precipitous dive sucking the purchasing power away from the consumer, the petrodollar system was created. Now with this new petrodollar system the world's consumers could now be enslaved by the U.S. central banks virtually worthless printed currency. Just to get another visual on how going from a gold standard to a fiat system has affected the value of the dollar, I am going to put a chart here again to remind you.

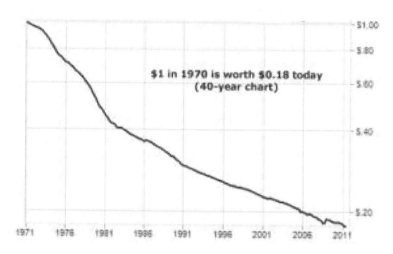

What the petrodollar system succeeded in doing is guarantee that the world would now have an essential need for the U.S. central banks fiat currency. Here is how it works. In return for U.S. military protection of their oil, the OPEC cartel would agree to price their oil in U.S. Dollars. What this means is that any nation wishing to acquire oil from OPEC would have to exchange their currency for U.S. fiat in order to purchase OPEC oil. Now with this petrodollar system a massive, sustained, and ever increasing global demand for the Fed's fiat was created, and subsequently because of this the dollar becomes the world's reserve currency. Admittedly this was true brilliance in action for by world's central bankers, they now can create unimaginable wealth by issuing debt to the world. Now that is greed in the extreme!

So, here we have the most powerful military the world has ever known protecting OPEC nations' oil. OPEC nations include Iraq, Kuwait, Libya, Saudi Arabia, United Arab Emirates, Qatar, Iran, Nigeria, Algeria, Angola, Ecuador, and Venezuela (12 nations). Let's look at this a bit more closely. We already have Iraq, Kuwait, and Libya under direct U.S. military control, that's 25% so far and there will be others in the near future. You would have to be blind to not see what is going on here. It is not enough that these countries had agreed to price their oil in the Fed's fiat. They, the politicocorporatists along with the MIC want control of the physical oil. I suppose the real question is this, why do they want control of the physical oil? Lets look at another chart.

World Population

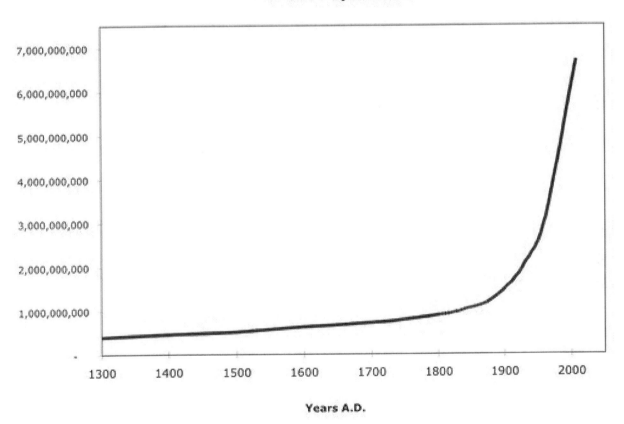

Years A.D.

The chart above demonstrates the world population boom which we are currently in, *this particular chart is a bit behind the times actually as we have just crossed the seven billion mark.*

55

However, what is important to be aware of here is it appears we are in a massive population bubble. The truth is yes, the exponential rise in the population is causing great strain on the world's natural resources. Which brings us back to why the politicocorporatists and the MIC want control of the physical oil. But before I elaborate on peak oil, I want you to look at another chart. This next chart demonstrates what has happened/is happening to the price of corn from March 2010 to April 2011. In one years time it has doubled in price. We all shop for food, so I do not have to tell you what is happening to the price of food items however, I will tell you that that these prices are going to get much higher. It is clear that commodities such as corn are going to be in an ever increasing demand as the world population continues to grow. The same is true for oil.

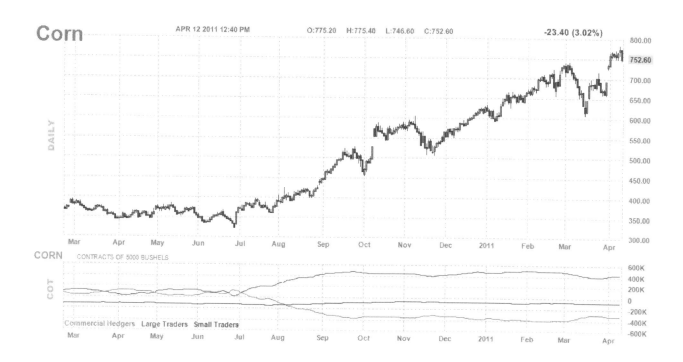

The Life Blood Of The Earth Is Oil

No single other item has influenced the world more than oil. Oil in many ways has taken us from the dark ages into our modern world. On average one 42 gallon barrel of oil creates 19.5 gallons of gasoline, and the rest is used to make other items. In fact thousands of common items are made from petrochemicals.

That Brings Us To This, Peak Oil

Is the world running out of oil? Probably not at this time. Perhaps someday there will be no oil left, however this may not occur for a very long time, how long? Who knows. Understand, I am not trying to make little of the situation and I do realize clearly that alternative sources of energy need to be explored. With that said the problem is not how much oil may or may not be left, its about how much is available and how quickly it can be pulled from the ground. That is the situation we are in right now. The demand for oil is frankly enormous, beyond enormous actually and growing every day. And at this time there is no clear solutions to keep up with this demand. Earlier I presented you with a chart showing the booming global population, much of that is from Asia. The demand for energy from Asia has now taken over the demand from the western world. The United States was the prime consumer of energy in the world, now it is Asia. The population boom is now in a positive feedback loop, growing populations begets an ever growing population exponentially. The swelling population of the Earth is in part due to people living longer because the the advancement of medicine, nutrition, among other things as well. But world population is also increasing because the birth survival rates are now much higher in the underdeveloped parts of the world. This positive feedback population boom is in a bubble, and at one point there will be a correction. Again it is the same situation, you have a population expanding at a rate far above what incomes, human resources, or global Gross Domestic Product dictates, therefore as in every other bubble it becomes and is not sustainable by any means.

We are already witnessing what strained natural resources are doing to the unfortunate peoples of third world countries, disease, starvation, and overall human suffering are at all time historic highs. And let me say this, as a provider of health care this is something that hits home for me.

Commodities Are Prophetic

Take a look at this chart.

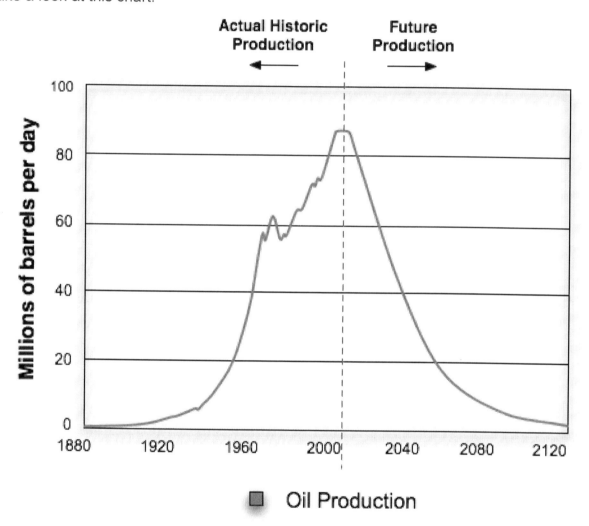

Oil Production

Can You Say Bubble?

Look at the run up in the production of oil from the 1920's until today. Peak oil is a term which is commonly used to define that point in time when the maximum rate of global oil extraction and therefore production is reached, after that time the rate of production enters terminal decline. A strong case can be made that we are in that period of time now. As we know the demand for oil is continuing to grow and has no chance of slowing until an alternative energy source is either discovered or created. The massive population boom/bubble at this time guarantees a massive and ever growing demand for oil. However is appears that with all the resources available to us at this time the extraction and therefore production of oil has peaked. From the 1930's up until the 1970's the extraction and production of oil rose steadily. Since that time the production of oil based upon demand has slowed dramatically, and without an alternative source of energy the gap between the production of oil verses demand is going to continue to widen.

The strain on natural resources is going on across the board, earlier I presented you with a chart demonstrating what is happening with the price of corn. I chose corn because thousands of commonly used items contain corn and the demand for more of it is only going to rise. The prices of all commodities have no where to go but up because of the population bubble, as well as the continued attack on the value of the dollar by the Federal Reserve as these items are priced in U.S. Dollars.

More Fear

As of late all we hear about by the main stream media is the threat Iran potentially poses by acquiring nuclear weapons. The politicocorporatists and the MIC it seems have chosen their next target yet another OPEC nation, and they are playing the fear card on not only the American common people but also the world's. They played the same card with the run up and subsequent Iraq war/takeover. Remember the whole weapons of mass destruction lie? The repeated showing of atomic explosions by the mainstream media?

How about how every member of the Bush administration would utter the words "mushroom cloud" whenever they had the chance on national television. How about how we were told of the undeniable proof regarding the existence of these weapons of mass destruction by British Prime Minister Tony Blair? I could go on and on but lets move to this: they recently got to take Libya by playing yet another set of cards.

The first card they played was rehashing the Lockerbie bomber's warm welcome when he returned to Libya causing people to get angry and wanting revenge. This "playing on the psyche" of the masses was being set up long before the actual "kinetic military action" as it was called. Oh yes, it was not a war because there was no American boots on the ground, another untruth by the way. American intelligence was on the ground months prior to the bombs being dropped and how do I know that? I was a military officer and I know how the system works, I am also very familiar with military tactics. The next folly card which was played by the MIC was this: *we have to drop an enormous amount of munitions on the Libyan government "for humanitarian reasons," because Qaddafi is turning his military on his own people.* Keep in mind that in Syria at this time the situation is much worse, the Syrian government right now as you are reading this is virtually exterminating the general public/any opposition to the status quo. Also keep in mind that Syria is not a member of OPEC, if they were, American bombers would now be in the skies over Syria, they would have to be. As you know the petrodollar accord states: the United States military must protect the oil of OPEC nations in order to preserve the U.S. Dollar as the world's reserve currency.

The Libyan Takeover

First they set up the "action" by creating global public anger at the Libyan government over the Lockerbie bomber, then they use the civil war in Libya as an excuse to go in and establish a military presence to take control of the physical oil. Very simple and straightforward.

Another reason Iran now has a target painted over it is this: Iran is the only OPEC nation which will sell its oil to another nation, namely Russia, not based in U.S. Dollars thus violating their petrodollar agreement. Currently we also understand that even other countries like Brazil, Russia, India, China, and South Africa, are also abandoning the U.S. Dollar in their trade as more nations begin to understand that the days of the U.S. Dollar being the world reserve are certainly numbered.

I am not sure if the main stream media is a party to all this manipulation or they are just literal talking heads being force fed whatever information they convey to the public. In any case there is very little real journalism anymore. There are some in the main stream media who I do respect greatly, for example Rick Santelli, and there are a few others. I often wonder how or even why some of those in the media got there in the first place? It is obvious that they have very limited insight about the issues which they "report on." As the day progresses sometimes on a minute to minute basis their story changes with the DOW, it is actually quite funny to watch.

With regard to the DOW, do you realize it has been basically flat since the year 2000? In the year 2000 we hit DOW 11,500 and today here at the end of 2011 it is, well actually a bit less that that. So all this talk of rally's, this or that with regard to the DOW is just fluff in an attempt to affect perception. Now if you priced the DOW against gold, the DOW has gotten slaughtered-but no one is reporting on that!

.

Section 4

A Financial Wrecking Ball Is Headed Our Way

The central banks, the politicocorporatists, and the Wall Street insiders are all keenly aware of the fact that the financial end game is at hand. However they don't really care and why is that? That is because all of them know how to "play the game." They are fully conscious of how this game will conclude and therefore they are positioning themselves accordingly and your turn is coming soon. My mission with the undertaking of this book project is to try my best and demonstrate to you as clearly as possible how important it is to know the parameters of this game, and I hope I have done that thus far. Now that you have an understanding of some of both the invisible and ominous factors involved in their **politicocorporatisticmilitarianism dogma,** *(a term I conjured up which encompasses the three major players in this economic mega game and their agenda),* and how it is more or less designed to keep the vast majority of people in a sheep like state, lets go back and look at a few charts and concepts. I have laid out these next few pages in kind of a time line manner for you. On the next page is the housing bubble chart.

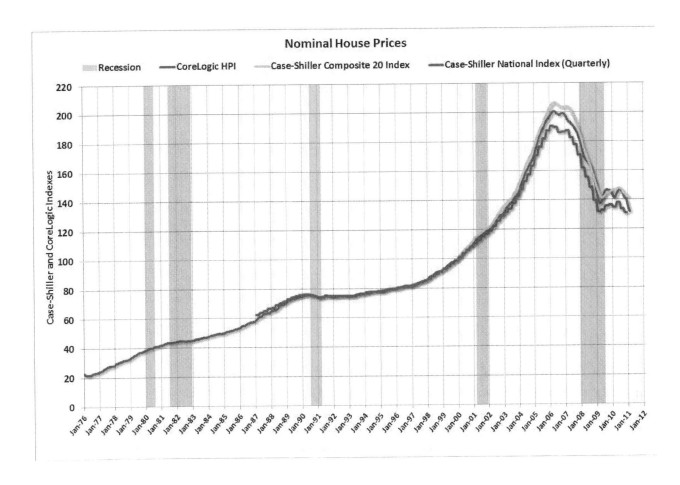

As we know, at this time the Fed. is in desperation mode made clear through the 300% increase in the monetary base in a futile attempt to stop the falling real estate market. The Fed. has also succeeded as well in bailing out the banks by purchasing tens of billions of toxic assets with tax payer cash. The Fed. is also subsequently, by printing more currency out of thin air, purchasing more long term treasury bonds in order to keep interest rates below fair market value. What the Fed. has done thus far is slow the drop in real estate by not allowing natural market dynamics to decide fair market value. In other words what Ben has succeeded in doing is not allowed a natural correction to occur at this point. Mr. Bernanke has also been successful in creating an ever swelling and gargantuan dollar bubble, the largest the world has ever known, and this can be visualized in this next chart.

63

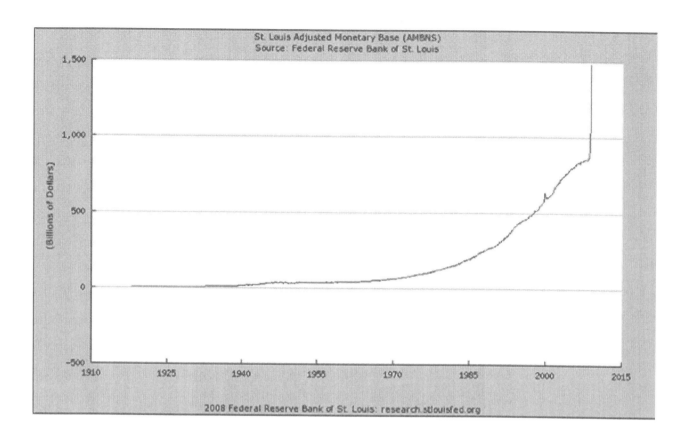

St. Louis Adjusted Monetary Base (AMBNS)
Source: Federal Reserve Bank of St. Louis

2008 Federal Reserve Bank of St. Louis: research.stlouisfed.org

This dollar bubble given to us again by the illustrious Ben Bernanke, has done this to the value of the dollar in one year.

Take a look at the chart below.

Now as we know, in order for Ben to keep this all going he has had to print fiat out of thin air and purchase treasury bonds in order to keep interest rates artificially low, purchasing these bonds also helps finance the day to day operations of the United States. This has caused yet another bubble to develop, and this bubble is THE MOTHER OF THEM ALL. It is the U.S. DEBT BUBBLE. Here is what it looks like, next page. (This chart does take the liberty of projecting what the debt will be in a year or two).

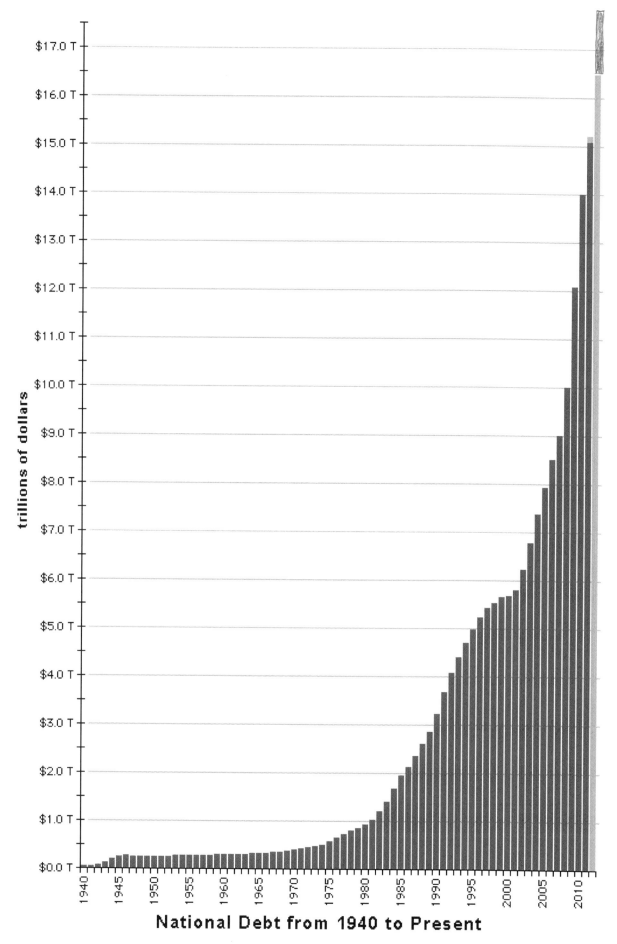

National Debt from 1940 to Present

Source: U.S. National Debt Clock
http://www.brillig.com/debt_clock/

Today the headlines read: "Stocks succumb to Europe," and "European Debt Crushed U.S. Markets," etc, etc. Never once do they mention that not only is the United States the biggest debtor nation in the history of the world with debt problems which eclipse that of Europe by exponents, problems which it will be facing in the near future. They, and you know who they are by now, are trying as hard as they can to cause it to seem like the United States is isolated from these problems and nothing could possibly be farther from the truth.

Well There It Is, The Mother Of All Bubbles

Just about a week ago the U.S. debt ballooned to near 15,900,000,000,000.00 (fifteen trillion nine hundred billion dollars), and now represents more than 104% of Gross Domestic Product (GDP). Interestingly, even though this is a grim historic event for the United States (crossing the 100% of GDP mark) it has gotten almost no media coverage, why do you think that is? Simple, it would affect consumer sentiment in a negative way. I believe a better way to think about the national debt is this: at this point in time the national debt is greater than seven times, actually closer to eight times, the total amount of tax revenue collected from the American people in a year and growing faster every day. The national debt is growing by about twenty five thousand dollars a second and this number will accelerate as the debt and subsequent interest accrue. Now lets say you are a lender, would you give a loan to any entity who's debt to income ratio was nearing 8 to 1 and growing with no end in sight? Not only is there no end in sight, the projections of where this galactic number will be going just over the next few years is staggering. In other words there is absolutely no possible way for the debt to be repaid and as soon as people get hip to that with a roar like thunder it is all coming down. Each week the government holds auctions for its treasury bonds, these bonds as you are aware finance everything that is needed to keep America running.

In Europe as of late the auctions for their bonds are not going so well, and because of that the yields on their bonds are moving higher and higher. The reason for that is as these bonds are perceived as riskier investments and in order for someone to buy them they expect a greater return on their asset's, very simple. Now here in the U.S. bond yields are at record lows for some of the reasons we have been covering, like the Federal Reserve buying them with printed out of thin air currency. The other reason is people still have their blinders on, therefore they continue to invest in long term U.S. bonds even though the interest earned by them is lower than the expected rate of inflation! That should explain to you how desperate the situation in Europe really is despite what you here in the main stream media.

Lets Talk A Little More About The U.S. Debt

Think about this a bit more for a moment, at just this point the tax revenue collected from the American people does not even cover the day to day expenses of running the country, it covers about 60% of them, the other 40% continues to be borrowed and this ratio is going to get much worse. Now again you are a loan officer, would you even remotely consider granting a loan to this client? I am sorry sir, but it seems you have run out of credit, have a nice day. Uncle Sam's pockets have been picked dry, and he has run up truly epic amounts of debt. Our country is completely broke and has to rely on other country's, investors, and the Federal Reserve as a lender of last resort to keep it propped up and running. I love this country, and as I sit here writing this trying desperately to warn as many people as I can of her impending collapse I honestly have to hold back tears. What a shame, what have we done? Are we all not a party to this action?

Collapse By Design?

There are those who believe that America is being caused to collapse deliberately, being brought forth by clandestine groups like the Illuminati for example. These individuals site certain symbols like these, (see image below), which can be found on any dollar bill however, I do not agree that by design America is being caused to collapse.

Some say it is the Free Masons whom are helping to destroy America. Freemasonry is an order which many of our founding fathers were a member to and still thrives today.

I believe it is generally easier for people to believe that some kind of grand, bordering on the supernatural scheme is responsible for the crisis we are in and subsequent ruination we are going to face, then to accept that natural forces combined with ineptitude, greed, and corruption are really to blame. The fall of the Soviet Union was brought about by the same triad, ineptitude, greed, and corruption. In a strange twist this is also true: *the bigger the lie the easier it is for people to believe it.*

The Wrecking Ball Cometh

The U.S. debt bubble can also be called the dollar bubble, which is likewise the bond bubble. All of these are three parts of the same thing and each is squarely dependent and an integral part of the other. The deficit which is the national debt is borrowed dollars, so here you have the connection between the debt bubble and the dollar bubble. The bond market represents IOU's, (to be paid with interest of course), which are also priced in dollars and added to the national debt, therefore as you can see each of these are a part of the same enormous three part mega bubble, and both you and I know what happens to economic bubbles. All economic bubbles without exception have to pop because they rise beyond levels which are able to be sustained by any means. *So as I have been saying throughout this book, whatever scheme the U.S. government, the Federal Reserve , the European Central Bank (ECB), the International Monetary Fund (IMF), the European Union (EU), or any governments act, or program attempts to do will fail over time, it is a mathematical certainty.*

I will repeat this again, all economic/financial bubbles cannot be sustained by ANY means. All that can be done is defer their inevitable bursting, and this postponement is the worst possible thing that can be done. All putting off or propping up the massive already hyper-inflated bubbles does is achieve in creating bigger, much more dangerous and devastating apocalyptic monster debt bubbles. These bubbles, the debt, dollar, and bond bubbles are going to pop and there is no question about it. Any argument to the contrary is simply utter nonsense as theses mega bubbles cannot be sustained by any means.

Now if the policymakers had the guts to make extreme cuts across the board beginning with slashing almost to non existence the entitlement programs, every piece of government pork, and stop policing the world while at the same time cutting taxes for the American people well then they can solve the problem. However that scenario has absolutely no chance of happening for several reasons most of which almost need no explanation, but the one reason which does warrant explanation and is not blatantly obvious is this: **the concept of greed to the extreme.** Please allow me to explain. I began this book project with the hope that I would be able to covey a message in such a way that it would allow people to have a better understanding of how this game is played. That I could just lay this all out in plain, clear, language which would enable anyone, not just someone with a PhD or a five hundred thousand dollar portfolio to grasp the folly which is being played on not just the American people, but the peoples of the world.

The Greatest Threat To Humankind

With that said: the policymakers, corporate insiders, and the Military Industrial Complex have twisted and allowed to happen the creation of the most monstrous threat to the peoples of the world, the three pronged unsustainable debt bubbles which include the national deficit, the dollar, and the bond market. This global debt issue must be understood for what is really is, if you were to weigh out the dangers posed against the peoples of the world with respect to what has the potential to affect more lives and cause more devastation across the board which would include famine and death, the elephantine global debt bubble is equally on par with a global nuclear exchange.

Is It Insanity Or Brilliance?

I suppose that depends of which side of the equation you are on, there are always two sides, but allow me to put a perspective on this. I am not a religious guy, but let's call the policymakers, corporate insiders, and the MIC collectively the "diabolical trinity," and this trinity has an agenda. On several occasions in this book I have eluded to the fact that the three main players in this game are positioning themselves for the fateful crash, for which you are now aware involves the three pronged mega bubbles bursting. What we are going to be doing is placing ourselves in much the same position as they, which is the opposite side of the equation unfortunately for the general uninformed public. Understand, there is no "lack of will" by the policymakers to change these things which is something we hear quite often in the main stream media. The politicians along with the other two participants which encompass this diabolical trinity at this point are being motivated by the end game, and greed is the main driver here. The diabolical trinity is well aware of this three pronged super bubble, and they are actually counting on its bursting sometime in the near future. In fact the bursting of these bubbles is the main facilitator of why they want to and are continuing to inflate it, and that is because the bigger they can make this bubble the more wealth they can create for themselves when it ultimately pops.

It basically comes down to a simple transaction, in fact the largest transfer of wealth the world has ever seen is already well underway and will begin to move with ever increasing speed as the three pronged debt bubble begins its downward trajectory. Of course the other side of the equation is this: that wealth they are banking on has to come from somewhere and it is going to be driven by fear to the extreme as the general population goes scrambling to sell all of their assets as their value plummets. Assets like real estate, 401K's, pension plans, equities, government bonds, are all going to suffer terrible and sustained losses because at this point they will have become toxic assets which is defined as *"assets whose value has fallen significantly and for which there is no longer a functioning market, so that such assets cannot be sold at a price satisfactory to the holder."*

72

What will then follow as the people who did not see this coming or chose not to heed warnings from people like myself and others will now have lost their faith **by force.** This will lead to mass "bank runs," and a vast majority of those seeking to withdraw their funds will get nothing. Even the FDIC (Federal Deposit Insurance Corporation) will not be able to help either as they too will be affected and have to declare bankruptcy, *within the confines of the situation presented.* And the (paper) wealth of the vast majority of the population of the United States and the world will be completely wiped out with no way for it to be recovered. Most people do not realize that the currency which "exists" in their accounts is actually not there, it exists as digital numbers only. All banks in order to make a profit have to lend out the cash they take in as deposits, and that currency is lent out on a multiplier. Here is how it works: You deposit $500.00 into one of your accounts, the bank is then allowed to multiply this deposit by a factor of ten and now is able to loan out $4,500.00. All banks and credit unions operate in this manner. A bank is only required to keep a fraction of its customers deposits on site, so in the event of a "bank run" as you can see, just a fraction of the depositors is going to get their fiat. As for the rest, destitution which will lead to desperation. This brings us back to the agenda of the fore aptly named diabolical trinity. Here is their agenda: as I stated earlier the wealth which will be lost by the general public is going to be "up for grabs" and collected by those who understand the rules and can play the game. As the three pronged bubble bursts and public assets become toxic panic will ensue and fear will create a mass wave of selling, and no one wants to be the last one out the door because there will be a point when there will be no buyers for these toxic assets. At this point even the Fed. will not be able to come to the rescue because the dollar bubble will have already burst, and massive and uncontrolled inflation will already be upon us. As aggregate public panic selling driven by fear continues, and the value of most assets across the board are plummeting, a massive transfer of wealth is going to be taking place. And the use of "mass" in this case is an grave understatement.

Keep in mind, all this fiat currency being created by the selling of these assets has to go somewhere and I will give you one guess who is going to be on the other side of this equation to collect it, yes, the diabolical trinity. **And you.** Understand this does not make you a bad person, at this point it is just the smart thing to do as you now have an understanding of how the end game is going to play out and you have every right to protect yourself and your family. I am going to detail in section 5 the necessary steps which you should be taking in order for you to capitalize of these sequences of events, but for now it is important to gain some more insight. Please keep in mind this is not personal, its business which we are talking about. You are not looking to screw anyone, it is about making the right decision based upon knowledge available to anyone, period.

What the Fed. has effectively done is create a dollar/bond/debt bubble of truly nightmare proportions. It is far and away the biggest bubble ever created by man. At this point in time with the European debt crisis in its early stages and what it appears as a successful campaign by the politicocorporatists in trying to keep the public eye off the ball, that is convincing the world that the United States is isolated from these debt issues, U.S. treasury bonds have been selling. In fact the rally in the bond market for someone like me who actually understands what is going on is baffling. However, I believe that it is fear which is the main driver here and fear causes rational people to do irrational things. Understand, these U.S. bonds are paying negative returns and are still being purchased at an ever increasing rate! That should give you an idea of how desperate and fearful people are regarding the European debt problem. Let's lay it all out on the table, what solutions do the European politicocorporatists have? They have only two. The first is to allow natural market forces to intervene which would cause immediate and massive asset losses across the board, or the second option: have the central banks fire up the printing presses and stave off the inevitable collapse for a few more years. Which one do you think they are going to choose?

By choosing option number two like the Federal Reserve already has, they will be successful in accomplishing a temporarily pushing off a much bigger and devastating collapse. What the central banks of the world are going to do beyond a shadow of a doubt is push this thing off as much as possible, and how they will do that is by printing massive amounts of fiat out of thin air. The farther they can push this off, because that is all they can do, the worse the inevitable collapse of the three pronged debt mega bubble is going to be. For those on the other side of the equation there is this: the more mass that can put into the debt, the greater the pay off is going to be. Understand in every game there are winners and there are losers, **it all boils down to a simple exchange.**

As this scenario plays out and we are seeing this happen now, there is going to be deflation, but this is just the initial phase. This deflationary period has no choice but to turn into massive inflation within a very short time, and this is because all this cash which the central banks are going to print is going to devalue the currency globally and exponentially. It is actually a bit more complicated than that however, Ben Bernanke believes that he can control inflation by contracting the currency supply. Ben falsely believes that other nations and investors are always going to want to own the dollar and U.S. Treasury bonds, he is very wrong. Even now countries and investors are distancing themselves from the dollar as we discussed earlier, the BRICS nations more specifically and the U.S. Dollar is losing its reserve status. Ben also fails to understand that with a national deficit of very near 16 trillion dollars investors will not want to buy and hold U.S. debt. Ben believes he will be able to sell the bonds he currently has on his balance sheet to contract the currency supply, but even now investors are getting negative returns on bond investments and soon they will realize there are much better places to put their cash. What this will do is force yields on these bonds higher which will subsequently push interest rates up. This will put major downward pressure on equity markets here in the U.S. and people will run for the door. Ben is not a trader, he is an economist, and therefore has a very poor understanding of how market and "money" dynamics work. Massive and even hyperinflation is coming, and it is the fault of Ben Bernanke and the Federal Reserve.

As we know the Federal Reserve has increased the monetary base 300% since 2008. However as of late we are not seeing any real inflation, yet. Part of the reason for this the Fed. is requiring banks to keep monies in reserve, which is something that is never done because if the banks do not loan out cash they make no profit. What the Fed. is doing in an attempt to control the flow of all this extra currency is paying the banks interest on the monies it keeps in reserve. What the banks are doing is keeping extra cash over and above their Fed. requirement in their reserves, because the Fed. is essentially paying them to do it. At this time it is in the banks' best interest to keep this extra cash in their reserves being that the Fed. is paying them interest on this currency, but for the economy this does not come without a price. It is actually a double edge sword, on one side of the equation having this extra cash in the banks' reserves keeps it from making its way out into the consumer side of the currency supply and causing inflation. But the other side of the equation is it keeps banks from lending, essentially freezing up consumer credit which keeps the economy from expanding. And of course the Fed. is paying the interest to the banks for their increased reserves with currency printed out of thin air, and what does this do? It continues to increase the monetary base and thus puts even more downward pressure on the value of the dollar.

The sluggish economy is also responsible for slowing the rate at which the Fed's liquidity enters circulation, this phenomenon occurs simply because people are not spending cash, or seeking loans. Therefore the extra "liquid" cash, stays out of the consumer side of the monetary base and there is no "money velocity."

At this point in time we are seeing the European bond yields rise and the U. S. bond yields drop. We are seeing this because the world still does not "get it" and realize that U.S. debt is not a safe haven. Sure the U.S. can pay back any debt which includes the deficit in full at anytime but it would have to do that by having Ben print it all out of thin air which would in turn reduce the dollar value to zero.

So it appears that Europe has just about maxed out their credit card and here in the U.S. investor fear of this European situation is still allowing us to acquire credit and therefore more debt. Judging from the bond rally as of late here in the U.S. I suspect this phenomenon will continue for a while longer. Today it seems people are losing interest in what they consider riskier assets namely the equity market and this is evident in the super low volume of trades however, they are willing to purchase treasury bonds which offer negative returns. What I know is there is no way the Federal Reserve is going to allow the equity markets or the real estate markets to collapse before increasing the monetary base a thousand percent more than the three hundred percent they already have. With this knowledge some equities are the place to be and not bonds which offer negative returns.

At some point the central banks are going to be "the lenders of last resort," and this will come about simply because those who were purchasing U.S. debt will have finally woken up to the fact that the debt can never be paid back, and at this point the end game will be imminent. Once the bond auctions begin to fail, and in Europe currently these auctions are already getting weaker, either the central banks have to step in and buy or the party is over. Again what do you think is the most likely scenario? In either situation interest rates will have to rise and this will push the recession button even harder, people will cut back on spending, businesses will close, unemployment will rise, less tax revenue will be collected, the central banks will have to print more fiat and the value of the currency will continue to decline. Because the central banks of the world will be printing fiat out of thin air for as long as they possibly can the astronomical three pronged debt bubble of the United States, and those in Europe will continue to inflate. At the point when the debt/dollar/bond bubble of the United States begins to collapse, something which is a mathematical certainty, every remaining bubble left on Earth will also simultaneously pop as well.

Section 5

There Is A Silver Lining

Having an understanding of how this game is going to play out gives us enormous opportunity. History has shown us that it is in times of great economic distress those who understand just a few basic rules make fortunes, and perhaps more importantly have survived. Being armed with an understanding of how the game works makes it easy for us to determine what actions by the governing bodies are going to be undertaken, and with this knowledge it is easy to make decisions. With this evolving and fast moving global financial crisis moving ever closer the time to place yourself into an adventitious position is now. The general public is woefully prepared for what is coming and that is because the American culture today virtually guarantees failure. Today far too many people are dependent on the government for their existence. Entitlement programs in this country have created legions of what would have been viable people who contribute to society in a meaningful way into people who have learned not to take care of themselves, and that is what scares me the most.

It is simple to deduce that there is no real or meaningful economic recovery here in the United States, and the global economy is showing ever increasing signs of great financial instability. I unfortunately believe that among developed nations the American public is going to suffer the most as this crisis deepens because so many are dependent on government support. The current situation is this: right now virtually anyone can put his or her self into a position in which a great deal of wealth will be made as this crisis develops. In fact there has never been a better time in the history of the world where an individual with little or no net worth at this time can become wealthy, there is a paradox here. While by and large the peoples of the western economies especially are going to be fleeced to the point of ridiculousness, some will reap incredible rewards in the form of financial well being.

Let's Talk

I hope that I have already established that the one place that you do not want to be is in cash, *that is unless you are an individual with experience in shorting bonds.* We know that the central banks of the world are going to print enormous amounts of fiat to try and stave off the popping of the debt/dollar/bond bubbles as long as possible and this is going to punish the value of currencies to the point of ridiculousness. We also know that as the three pronged bubble's inevitable fall accelerates global bond yields are going to rise dramatically. The Fed. has made it clear that they are going to keep interest rates at these artificial/historic lows until at least 2013, what happens then? The Fed. cannot lower rates any more, as we already know the yields of long term treasuries is negative so the only way interest rates have to go is up. At one point no matter how or what the Fed. or other world central banks do it will be the market that dictates fair market value with regard to interest rates and what we may see at that point is an uncontrolled, rapid rise in these rates due to uncontrollable fear which is going to pervade the bond market. As treasury bonds sell off and interest rates rise the equity markets too are going to sell off and I believe rapidly at this point. With the sell off in equities and T-bills, (Treasury Bonds), this extra cash is going to look for a place to go and that place is into commodities. At this point in the sequence the already rising commodity prices are going to spike across the board and inflation is going to make it very difficult for people to obtain even basic necessities. I am certain that the biggest spike in commodity prices is going to be in crude oil and precious metals. Now if you are a savvy trader with a lot experience in these things, an excellent position for you to be in at this point in the sequence would be short positions almost across the board but especially bonds and financial stocks. If you are just the average Joe you should be taking up long positions in commodities, especially energy and mining companies. If you are even less savvy than the average Joe and only have a small, or almost no amount to invest no worries, I have a plan for you as well which I will elaborate on later.

Take a look the chart below. What this chart demonstrates is the DOW/Gold ratio over time, (since1900). As you can see there are repeating phases here, that is there are times in which the price of one ounce of gold equals the DOW.

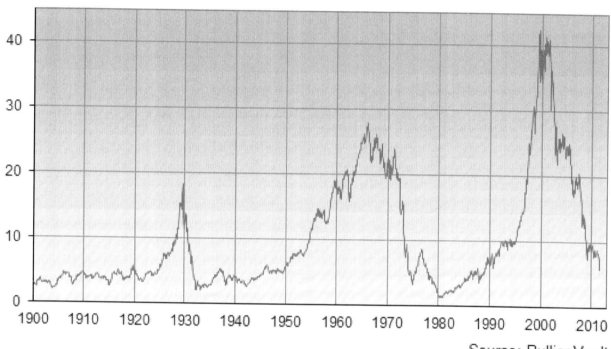

Dow/Gold Ratio (monthly)

Source: BullionVault

Do you see a pattern here?

It appears that we are now nearing a position in this sequence where the Dow/Gold ratio is going to correct to one to one. However, we are in no ordinary times right now and I believe we are going to correct better than the one to one ratios which this chart is historically demonstrating and an over-correction is going to take place. At a minimum sometime in the near future this ratio will be at least one to one, but I believe almost beyond any doubt that fear and greed are going to push this ratio to better than the historic one to one.

The main driver here is going to be all these dollars fleeing the bond markets which will cause yields and interest rates to rise, this in turn will put massive downward pressure on the equity's markets. As the equity's markets along with the bonds fall the price of gold will rise until the historic one to one ratio is achieved however, we have never been in a situation like the current financial crisis. We are in the midst of a massive debt/dollar/bond bubble and when this bubble pops the Fed. will be almost powerless to stop it therefore again, I am expecting to see an over-correction. Why I am saying the Fed. will be "almost" powerless to stop it? Because there is one thing the Fed. can do, and that one thing would be to peg the dollar to a hard asset like gold. However by the time the Fed. would even consider pegging the dollar to an asset like gold the price would have probably more that quadrupled from where is it today which is about $1,600.00 an ounce. In fact I am just about certain that gold in any situation is going to go much higher than quadruple today's price. I will also say something else, I believe that as this situation plays out we are going to be seeing a dramatic discrepancy between the commodities exchange (COMEX) spot price or "paper" gold and the bullion price, the same goes for silver. What is going to drive the price differential between spot and bullion is this: fear. Fear is going to cause a massive, sustained, and increasing demand for gold *and silver* and this demand is quickly going to overwhelm the supply which the COMEX claims it has. Once the COMEX becomes overwhelmed and cannot deliver on the orders being placed for physical delivery of the metals, bullion prices are going to rise exponentially.

***I am certain beyond any doubt that the next bubble which is going to be created is a gold super bubble, you can quote me on this and I believe I am the first to be publishing this prediction. Lets see if I am right! The popping of the three pronged debt bubble (deficit/dollar/bond) is going to cause a major downward correction in every asset class across the board, (except commodities, especially oil and precious metals). However, fear is going to cause an over-correction.

The reason why I keep bringing up my theory of an over-correction is because at that point, and this expands upon my gold super bubble theory, we are going to want to get our cash out of certain asset's and into the distressed assets which are going to be created by the bursting of the three pronged mega bubble and this is how we are going to create our dynasty.

Don't Buy Gold

As we know asset bubbles are a common part of history and when the debt/dollar/bond bubble deflates it is going to create yet another bubble, a super bubble I believe, and that bubble is going to be a gold super bubble. This next super bubble is going to create massive wealth for those who understand how this financial crisis is going to play out. However I am not advocating that you invest in gold, I am advising you to invest in silver instead. Is there anything wrong with buying gold? Absolutely not, and if you do buy gold you will make huge profits but consider this. The silver to gold ratio currently is about 57 to 1, and historically this ratio is about 15 to 1, what this means is at this time silver is grossly undervalued and promises to outperform gold in terms of return on your investment. In the midst of the gold super bubble which I am predicting, the multiples created by holding silver are going to be staggering.

Take a look at the chart below.

Dow/Gold Ratio (monthly)

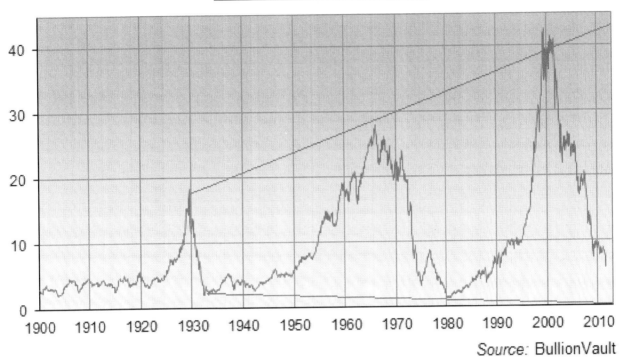

Source: BullionVault

This chart is again the DOW/gold ratio over time however, in this particular chart I have included trend lines at both the peaks and troughs. It is easy to get a visual on where is appears this is going. It also appears that this ratio will indeed be better than one to one favoring gold. It is no secret that central banks of the world who for the past several decades have been net sellers of gold are now acquiring it in mass. In fact never before in history since the inception of central banking has their been a time in which the accumulation of gold by these institutions has been so great.

Question: Do you think they know something which they do not want the general population to know?

Answer: Without a doubt yes.

Fact: *if people simply instead of depositing their paychecks of the Federal Reserve's fiat paper just took a percentage of that paper cash and converted in into real money like gold or silver, instead of becoming poorer each day the Fed. prints more of their counterfeit money they would be getting richer. This also has another beneficial effect, each time someone exchanges their fake paper wealth for real wealth in the form of gold and silver they take power away from the central bankers. It is the easiest thing to do and you would be creating real wealth for yourself while at the same taking it away from the central bankers.* (And this should be your counter-action to the Fed's policy of devaluing the dollar.)

At the beginning of this segment I started off with "don't buy gold," I really did not mean you shouldn't buy gold. Buying gold, or to put it another way exchanging the Federal Reserve's fiat paper for real money like gold is without a doubt one of the best things that you can do to create wealth in the coming years however it is not the best thing.

Accumulate As Much Silver As You Can Possibly Get Your Hands On

As you know I am predicting the next bubble right here and now, and that is going to be a gold super bubble driven by people having lost their faith in this fake, fiat, Ponzi scheme based economy. The loss in faith is going to be brought forth by the popping of the three pronged debt/dollar/bond bubble of which is a mathematical certainty because they cannot be sustained by any means.

OK, so what else do we know? The DOW/Gold ratio will correct to at least one to one, although I am predicting better than that in favor of gold. So that poses this question: how low is the DOW going to go? Before I answer that question let's be mindful that the Fed. is at some point is going to initiate another form of quantitative easing, actually at the time of this writing the Fed. has just begun the second round of operation twist as well as using nearly another 300 billion to purchase long bonds, which will serve once again in creating an even more massive debt/dollar/bond bubble.

How big can this get? Frankly who knows, but the bigger it gets the more punishment is going to be forced upon the general public and this beating is going to be severe. The other thing we know is this: as the endgame plays out the Fed. is going to be forced to purchase an ever increasing amount of U.S. Treasury bonds simply because countries like China and India who are at this time are the largest purchaser of U.S. debt, will simply say enough is enough and buy no more. Understand, the current U.S. bonds being held not just by China and India but all of them in their entirety are not going to be paid back, there is no way America can do it. Therefore the debt is in a massive ultra-bubble which cannot be sustained by any means. In fact, the U.S. deficit is the biggest 'bad loan" in the history of humanity.

The other factor which the Chinese as well as all the countries which now hold U.S. Treasury bonds are well aware of is this: due to the monetizing of the debt by the Fed. any monies which in theory "could" be paid back would be done so with devalued currency. What this means is every single entity, government or otherwise, which now holds a United States Treasury bond is guaranteed to lose cash on these said bonds because the Fed. has taken purchasing power out of the dollar! Now at some point in the not so distant future when the debt/dollar/bond bubble pops, whatever the eventual astronomic number may be at that time, it all becomes PAYMENT DUE IN FULL. So what happens then? Obviously America does not have the wealth to pay it back, so default occurs. Even if Ben were to crank up every printing press he has, and even builds more in an attempt to monetize the debt in total in order to pay our creditors the effect will be the same. A worthless or near worthless currency. It is this scenario, a debt default by the United States which is a mathematical certainty that is going to be responsible for and create the gold super bubble I am predicting. Now all this leads us back to the question I posed earlier which was: how low is the DOW going to go? I will answer that question now. In 2007 the DOW hit a high of 14,164, much of this was fueled by the housing bubble which allowed our economy to boom beginning sometime in the mid 1980's when the DOW was around 1,500.

So we now know that the housing bubble has burst and subsequently the drivers of that bubble are now gone. We now have high unemployment and are continuing in somewhat of a deflationary environment, except for food and energy. The prospects for real economic growth are bleak at best, because without some kind of catalyst to get the economy back on track we are just about dead in the water. Now if the Federal Reserve would have not intervened with QE1, then QE2 and increasing the monetary base 300% since 2008, all of this would have already corrected to fair market value and at this point in time and although we would still be hurting to some extent our wounds would have begun to heal. It is exceedingly difficult to put a number on how low the DOW will go, however we can by taking several factors into the equation guesstimate. We hit a high of around 14,000 in late 2007, and the low since that time was around 6,500 in early 2009, then the Fed. stepped in with QE effectively putting a halt to natural market drivers. Consider this, when we had a free market, *something which the Federal Reserve has ended by direct intervention as I have detailed throughout this book,* it was the market's sole job to determine fair market value. In essence the Fed. is telling the investing world as a whole that they know better and subsequently had to step in and save the markets, a very dangerous and portentous thing indeed. In 2007 when the market peaked the national debt was around ten trillion, it is 33% larger now and growing rapidly. Also at that time the monetary base was over 300% less. In 2009 the national debt grew to around twelve trillion and the Fed. had increased the monetary base by the fore mentioned 300%. We now have a national deficit at nearly sixteen trillion which also exceeds 104% of GDP. Prior to all this market manipulation by the Fed., a prediction on where the DOW may have bottomed out would have been much easier, and I would say a good guess would have been somewhere around 5,000, but now it is way tougher to make an accurate prediction but I am going to anyway. I would say based on the information at this time a good guesstimate in my opinion would be DOW 4,000. It could go less because of a fear driven over-correction, possibly as low as DOW 3,500, but understand I am making these guesstimates based on the bursting of the three pronged super bubble scenario which I elaborated on at length earlier on.

I realize this is a very stark outlook, believe me, but consider the fact that before the Fed. stepped in with QE the DOW had hit 6,500 the economy was in much better shape than it is now and there was no panic selling. So what does this mean for gold? As I have been saying I sincerely believe that the next super bubble is going to be in gold. I also affirm that the DOW/Gold ratio will correct better that one to one. I believe we are going to see gold go to 2X the value of the DOW at minimum, so my prediction for gold is going to be somewhere around $8,000 an ounce, could it go even higher? Sure, but that is my prediction. What does this mean for crude? Also a massive spike. I started off this segment with: *Accumulate as much silver as you can possibly get your hands on,* and here is where the real cheesecake is going to be. Silver is the investment of the century and this is where just about anyone can get in on this game.

Today the spot price of silver is around $28.00 which puts the silver/gold ratio at about 57 to 1. Historically this ratio is 15 to 1, I am sure you can see where I am going with this. Gold is going to be the next super bubble topping out at around $8,000, of this I have no doubt. If silver were to just attain its historic norm of 15 to 1 we are looking at a spot price of silver of around $500 an ounce however, I believe that this ratio is going to be closer to 10 to 1 before this all plays out and I will tell you why. As we know supply, demand, and human perception are the main market drivers in asset price, I have gone over that at length. Gold and silver are exceedingly rare and as such they are priced accordingly based in U.S. Dollars. We also know that central banks have been net buyers of gold for the last 4 years, something which has not occurred in decades as central banks are generally net sellers of gold. Countries around the world who have had gold stored here in the United States are now repatriating their gold from the U.S. This repatriation of gold by countries around the world from the U.S. is now common knowledge, therefore you can see clearly that they too are preparing for some major future event.

The reason I believe that silver is going to correct better than its historic norm is this, it's cheap, much cheaper than gold, and when people get wind of this they are going to sell everything including the kitchen sink rushing to get some. There are going to be supply concerns which I believe will not be able to keep up with demand, and the perception that silver is a "must have" by the general public is going to start a buying frenzy and at that point in time public perception regarding silver would be 100% correct. Right now virtually anyone can afford silver as the spot price is about $28.00 an ounce, not so much for gold. Plus people are not that stupid and eventually they are going to wake up to the fact that with regard to the silver to gold ratio, silver is more than a bargain which promises to pay off huge when this all plays out.

There are a total of 535 Members of Congress, one hundred serve in the U.S. Senate, while 435 serve in the U.S. House of Representatives, of these 47% are millionaires. Tell me, where do you think they are keeping their wealth? In cash? Absolutely not. How about big business? They all have massive portfolios and they too are net buyers of gold, although they do have legions of very savvy traders taking both long and short positions on equities, I should know, I used to be one of them. So now you are aware of where the politicocorporatists, the central banks, and even foreign countries are putting their cash.

Despite what the talking heads on the television are saying regarding the price of gold, this is what is driving the price, a limited supply and increasing demand. At the beginning of this book I began by elaborating on human behavior and perception, how fear and greed often forces an asset's price beyond that what fundamental or technical factors would dictate, well here is where that all comes into play. Having an understanding based on historical data in conjunction with the typical behavior of human beings during these times makes it easy to predict the most likely outcomes. I hope I have convinced you by presenting you with a logical explanation that the next super bubble is going to be gold, however I am suggesting that you buy silver.

Earlier on I discussed the current and historic ratios between the two precious metals, currently 57 to 1, historically 15 to 1. What this tells us is that no matter what happens to gold, silver will outperform gold over time. And here is the beauty of it, at this time virtually anyone can afford to exchange some of the Fed's fiat for real money, *silver.* There are several reputable companies which will sell you precious metals, go online, check it out, do a little research into the company's and find the one that is best for you. Precious metals are the easiest thing to not only accumulate but to sell as well. If you choose, all of the companies which sell these metals also buy them. You can also sell them to anyone who may want to buy them from you. I am also going to let you in on a little secret, heck we are friends now right? When you sell your precious metals you do not have to pay capital gains tax. I want you to re-read the previous sentence and focus on these two words, **have** and **to**, you figure out the rest.

Moving On

What you, me, the politicocorporatists, central banks, and various countries in the world are now waiting for is the gold super bubble, and we are going to take advantage of that by accumulating as much silver as we can get our hands on. We are going to in essence become our own central banks, we are going to preserve and create wealth for ourselves by accumulating silver. Right now gold and especially silver, judging with the knowledge we have now, are at fire sale prices beyond a shadow of a doubt. As the three pronged bubble collapses we are going to witness the largest transfer of wealth the world has ever seen and at the end of this there will only be two classes of people, the upper class and the lower class, *the middle class will be gone.* Which class do you want to be? Its up to you at this point. So now that I have outlined the first step of how you and I are going to begin to create wealth, wait, you thought I was done? No no, that's just half the story.

After The Endgame

Let's call this section, overtime. By this point if you have heeded my advice, that means you would have played your cards just right. Now what do we do? Simple. When this gold super bubble has played out, at or near the top of the spike when there is still huge demand for our silver it will then be time to sell our precious metal, a sad time indeed. *You didn't think you were going to keep it forever now did you?* So you have accumulated silver and now the end game in metals is here. Hypothetically, let's say you had acquired 500 troy ounces of silver bullion by this time and the gold super bubble tops out at $7,654.00 an ounce. Now let's also low ball it and say silver made it just to its historical norm ratio of 15 to 1 (as you know I am predicting 10 to 1), you now have an amount of silver worth $255,133.00 Time to say goodbye to our beautiful shiny metal as this party has ended, the gold super bubble has topped out and we have succeeded in our plan. What we are going to do at this point is put our newly acquired wealth into one or more distressed assets which will be abundantly available at that time. When everybody went scrambling for an exit as their assets value plummeted, that over-correction in the real estate and equity markets had occurred, *and that* is where we want to put our new cash to work!

Let's look at the dollar bills symbolism again just for a moment.

I want you to look at the pyramid for a moment, observe how the top portion is disconnected from the bottom section, **these proportions are correct.** After all this is said and done the ones who aware, the ones on top, are going to be the winners of this game and the ones below moving ever closer to the bottom are going to be the woeful losers.

America's Debt/War Based Economy

Before I end this book I thought that it would be important to speak a little more about how our "debt based/war based economy" functions. As we know since going off the gold standard in 1971 the value of the dollar has been in a downward trajectory, continually sucking more and more purchasing power from every person/country/entity who currently is holding our debt based fiat. (Holders of the dollar are also those who purchase/hold U.S. treasury bonds or any dollar derivatives). Before we were taken off the gold standard in a stealthy calculated move between the MIC, OPEC, and the U.S. policymakers, we did not have a debt based economy, what we had was an economy built upon the creation of wealth for the U.S. citizens and our country as a whole, America was truly the land of opportunity. The Constitution of the United States notes explicitly that all monies created (printed or otherwise) be backed by an equal amount of gold and or silver, in fact there is no amendment to the Constitution which allows for a fiat, or debt based monetary system. Therefore It could be considered that what the Federal Reserve does/is doing by issuing debt as money is "counterfeiting." Debt based economies which is unfortunately the model for most of the world is the root cause of the debt problems being faced by the world today, the debt crisis. If we/the world did not have debt based economies none of the problems facing the world with regard to sovereign debt would exist. Think of it this way, during the gold standard when an individual earned currency in reality they were receiving gold, the paper currency issued represented real wealth which was the gold and silver stored in government stockpiles therefore, during the gold standard the government and the Federal Reserve did not issue debt, it issued real wealth. Today because of our fiat monetary system the only thing which is issued by the Federal Reserve in the form of fake fiat counterfeit money is debt. Each bill/coin issued represents debt owed back to the Federal Reserve plus any accrued interest. The central banks of the world all work in the same manner, they issue public debt which creates private wealth for themselves.

What the Federal Reserve does is criminal plain and simple. The Fed. literally prints currency out of thin air and then distributes that created fiat backed by nothing which is then owed back to them with any accrued interest in the form of debt. The Federal Reserve is the biggest counterfeiter on the Earth. It is also the Fed. who is responsible for the three pronged debt/dollar/bond mega bubble we are in right now, something I have elaborated on at length in the text. The entire fiat monetary system of the United States was created for one purpose in collusion between the world's central bankers and the Military Industrial Complex, and that purpose is **WAR**. I have elaborated on several occasions in this book the real reasons why we were taken off the gold standard, it is a very simple and straightforward concept. The central bankers/Federal Reserve in direct collusion with the Military Industrial Complex wanted to create a fiat monetary system and there reasons were twofold: first, a fiat monetary system would allow the Federal Reserve to now create mass public debt while at the same time creating mass private wealth for themselves, wealth beyond imagination. Think about it for a moment, every dollar held by all of America's people, rich and poor alike, digital or printed, as well as every government backed bond/dollar derivative etc. etc is actually owned by the Federal Reserve. So every dollar in existence is "owned" and "owed back" to the Federal Reserve plus interest. Now that is incredible, don't you think? The second reason for the creation of a fiat monetary system is so there would be a literal endless supply of cash available to fight any and all wars the MIC would choose to fight then, (the Vietnam war), and any other war in in the future. So each dollar in your pocket or bank account is an IOU, made payable directly to the Federal Reserve plus interest. It must be understood that the business of WAR is the single largest generator of monies on the Earth, the cost of war in dollars is staggering. In fact the sole reason why the dollar is now the world's reserve currency, as discussed in the text, is the OPEC nations agreed to price their oil in U.S. Dollars in exchange for military protection of that said oil, (the petrodollar accord).

The true reason why we fought the Vietnam war was to first establish a fiat monetary system and second, to create the petrodollar system. Do you think it was just coincidence that we went off the gold standard at the same time the petrodollar system was created? And we went off the gold standard to finance the Vietnam war. Think about this for a moment, if America was not involved in some type of military conflict many of America's biggest corporations would not exist. These companies which create weapons of war such as Boeing, Lockheed Martin, Grumman, General Dynamics, etc. etc., (there are thousands of corporations spanning the globe which supply and create high tech weaponry, aircraft, ships, munitions, and all manner of war sustaining/fighting equipment) and all of them have a vested interest in the generation and expansion of war. It is also no secret that all these corporations are major contributors to America's policymakers to the tune of tens of billions or dollars. For our policymakers it is their interests, *the interests of the corporations especially the ones which sustain war which are important*, not those of you or I.

My Grandfather used to say "money talks and shit walks," and it took me a long time to figure out what that meant but I think I got it now. Every war fought by the United States after WWII has been one of choice, not necessity. Of all the nations on the Earth the United States has the largest global military presence, and America also holds the record with regard to the amount of military campaigns fought by any civilized nation, do you now understand why? Our current debt based economy is designed to create debtors, not wealth, and war, not peace.

Financial Stability Or Indentured Servants?

Very briefly, who are the IMF (International Monetary Fund) and the World Bank? In 1944 in what was known as the Bretton Woods agreement the IMF and World Bank were created. These institutions are complex and I will not elaborate on how they are structured however, their mission is stated as to foster global financial stability, monitor global economies as to not allow situations to be created which could possibly lead to monetary dysfunction as in the stock market crash of 1929. Their mission also includes offering loans to already impoverished nations and financial assistance, also in the form of loans to nations requiring it. So what they try to do is solve debt problems by adding more debt, just like the Federal Reserve does as well as the European Central Bank is trying to do in Europe right now. With a show of hands how many of you believe you can solve a debt problem by adding more debt!? OK, so the BIS, IMF, World Bank, ECB and the Fed. all have the same mission, and that is to again foster financial stability globally-In this mission they all have failed miserably, that is if you actually believe that is their mission. All of these institutions are creators of debt and debtors, not wealth. Their sole job is to enslave the world through and with debt. Understand, each of these institutions are privately owned and they are not non-profit. These organizations (cartel), serve to create profit for those individuals which own them, basically private banks. Each of these organizations are responsible for the galactic global debt crisis we are now in the midst of and it is also they who are acquiring gold in mass as of late. Does this seem strange to you? The very organizations which create mass public debt on a global scale are now net buyers of gold. As I have stated several times in this book, these entities are very well aware that the global debt issues/crisis cannot be fixed by any means, and it is also they who are continuing to inflate the gargantuan debt bubbles of not just the United States but the world. If you retain anything from this book let it be this: a popping of the three pronged debt bubble which we have gone over at length in this book is a mathematical certainty, and it is deliberately continuing to be fueled with purpose: **to bring about the greatest transfer of wealth the world has ever seen**-And I want you to be on the winning side.

Section 6

Global Financial Impact

Today we stand peering into a global financial and economic abyss the likes of which has never been seen before in human history. We are all stealthily being pushed ever closer to an inevitable economic and financial meltdown on a world wide scale by those who control everything. Be not mistaken my friend, this push is deliberate and being done with a clear purpose. What is this purpose? Ah yes! To continue to facilitate the greatest transfer of wealth the world has ever seen! The grandest of all thievery which is being done in plain sight yet so few even realize it is happening. The vast scope of this fast approaching inevitable event and its ramifications for the human race is truly staggering.

Simultaneously and globally we are witnessing the death of the debt based economic model built around a fiat or fake monetary system. A system that has caused the peoples of the world to believe that numbers printed on pieces of paper represent real money and hold actual value. In truth this is nothing more than a false impression which has been propagated by governments and run by central bankers. In actuality the value of these papers with numbers printed on them is nothing more than grand illusions which right now as you are reading this paragraph is fading with ever increasing speed. The end of this system which is based upon the continual and relentless accumulation of debt on a global scale began at its inception. The gross over-leveraging by governments and financial institutions has virtually assured an uncontrolled collapse of the entire monetary system. It is not a question of if, but simply when. What is continuing to be done by the governments of the world in a futile attempt to keep this debt acquisition in perpetuity scheme going is this: even more debt is being added at incredible rates. The central banks of the world have now become lenders of last resort. Understand: if nations cannot sell their bonds and thus accumulate even more debt the whole system collapses overnight.

All modern economies are solely based upon the acquisition of debt into infinity, and as such are destined to fail. Once no more debt can be acquired by a nation's government a "debt crisis" ensues. The issue is really not so much debt; It is an issue of solvency, or the inability to pay back the monies borrowed by the governments of the world. Modern governments of the world who each now rely on this system, a debt based economic model, are all entirely bankrupt and have absolutely no ability to repay the staggering amounts of debt they have accumulated. At this time no nation on Earth is in a worse state of affairs with regard to this debt issue than that of the Untied States. Furthermore the currency globally is simply this: unbacked liabilities being distributed by bankrupt governments and the world's central banks. The fact that people simply accept that this paper has real value is the sole reason why they are willing to work for it. What we are now in the very early stages of on a global level of this, a transition period. A transition from a global debt based economic model based upon fake money to a new system based upon a return to sound money (backed by a hard asset with real value) which will once again ensure wealth for all as opposed to the few. The adaptation of a debt based economic model promises one thing, at the point when no more debt can be added a crisis will occur, this is a mathematical certainty and we are all at that point right now.

These are truly historic times we are living through, so open your eyes and take a good look around because the world which you have come to know is going through a metamorphosis, one which is going to affect every human being on the planet. America's run as the number one global economic engine is coming to an abrupt end. The United States was once the richest nation on the globe and has now become the world's biggest debtor nation, the consequences of this are soon to be revealed with far reaching and devastating global financial/economic impacts.

"Societies are based upon perception and deception, and it is these two principles which are the driving forces propelling the peoples of nations by their leaders."
Gregory Mannarino.

For those who govern societies there are three main principles which have proven themselves to be true, and these are *ineptitude*, *greed*, and *corruption*. The perception of the people is contorted into their reality specifically by those who govern, and this system has again proven to be the destroyer of nations. Governments of the world have in collusion with central bankers and corporate insiders created a system in which war is being waged against citizens in an attempt to strip them (us) of our wealth, in fact a redistribution of that said wealth on an unimaginable scale.

This system is in reality creating slaves willing to work for nil, giving them (us) nothing but pieces of paper with numbers printed on them which have no real value because they are backed by nothing. The creation of "currency from nothing" has become the basis of this Grand Illusion and has allowed global debt based economic models to emerge worldwide. This framework has created a debt based economic model based on a "fiat" or "fake" monetary system, and this has now become the standard for the "civilized" world. This system is not just a Grand Illusion, but Grand Theft on an almost inconceivable scope. In fact it is on a scale so great that to put this into perspective think about this: the richest 1% of the people in the United States hold half the countries wealth.

What must be understood is the Central Banks of the world which includes the Federal Reserve are not government entities, they are privately owned and they operate for profit despite their claims to the contrary. The world's central banks who are responsible for global monetary policy are privately owned for profit institutions period. So tell me, who's interests do they support? The public or that of their shareholders/owners? The answer is quite obvious.

The world's central banks serve the interests of Wall Street. In fact the world's central banks are a business enterprise monopoly controlled by Wall Street. Wall Street buys and pays for political influence across the board. Presidential candidates receive tens of millions in contributions by Wall Street institutions as does nearly every member of Congress here in the United States. Barack Obama's 2008 campaign netted 16 million dollars from Wall Street firms, such as Goldman Sachs, Bank of America, Citigroup, UBS AG, JP Morgan Chase, and Morgan Stanley. It is also these same Wall Street firms who continue to "pay off" virtually every member of Congress as well as political leaders of every country in the world to further their agenda. Is it any surprise to you that it is these same institutions which get bailed out for making bad bets in "investments" using tax payer monies?

The following is a list of banks which got bailed out, (had their bad bets made whole), under the TARP program. The shaded areas denote those banks who either have, or are in the process of repaying their bailout monies to the Treasury.

Date	Bank	City	State	Amount
10/28/2008	Wells Fargo & Co.	San Francisco	Calif.	$25,000,000,000
10/28/2008	State Street Corp.	Boston	Mass.	$2,000,000,000
10/28/2008	Bank of America Corp.1	Charlotte	N.C.	$15,000,000,000
10/28/2008	JPMorgan Chase & Co.	New York	N.Y.	$25,000,000,000
10/28/2008	Citigroup Inc.	New York	N.Y.	$25,000,000,000
10/28/2008	Morgan Stanley	New York	N.Y.	$10,000,000,000
10/28/2008	Goldman Sachs Group Inc.	New York	N.Y.	$10,000,000,000
10/28/2008	Bank of New York Mellon Corp.	New York	N.Y.	$3,000,000,000
11/17/2008	Regions Financial Corp.	Birmingham	Ala.	$3,500,000,000
11/17/2008	UCBH Holdings Inc.	San Francisco	Calif.	$298,737,000
11/17/2008	Bank of Commerce Holdings	Redding	Calif.	$17,000,000
11/17/2008	Broadway Financial Corp.	Los Angeles	Calif.	$9,000,000
11/17/2008	SunTrust Banks Inc.	Atlanta	Ga.	$3,500,000,000
11/17/2008	Northern Trust Corp.	Chicago	Ill.	$1,576,000,000
11/17/2008	Provident Bancshares Corp.	Baltimore	Md.	$151,500,000
11/17/2008	U.S. Bancorp	Minneapolis	Minn.	$6,599,000,000
11/17/2008	TCF Financial Corp.	Wayzata	Minn.	$361,172,000
11/17/2008	BB&T Corp.	Winston-Salem	N.C.	$3,133,640,000
11/17/2008	1st FS Corp.	Hendersonville	N.C.	$16,369,000
11/17/2008	Valley National Bancorp	Wayne	N.J.	$300,000,000
11/17/2008	KeyCorp	Cleveland	Ohio	$2,500,000,000
11/17/2008	Huntington Bancshares	Columbus	Ohio	$1,398,071,000
11/17/2008	Umpqua Holdings Corp.	Portland	Ore.	$214,181,000
11/17/2008	First Horizon National Corp.	Memphis	Tenn.	$866,540,000
11/17/2008	Comerica Inc.	Dallas	Texas	$2,250,000,000
11/17/2008	Zions Bancorporation	Salt Lake City	Utah	$1,400,000,000
11/17/2008	Capital One Financial Corp.	McLean	Va.	$3,555,199,000
11/17/2008	Washington Federal Inc.	Seattle	Wash.	$200,000,000
11/17/2008	Marshall & Ilsley Corp.	Milwaukee	Wis.	$1,715,000,000
11/21/2008	City National Corporation	Beverly Hills	Calif.	$400,000,000
11/21/2008	Pacific Capital Bancorp	Santa Barbara	Calif.	$180,634,000
11/21/2008	Heritage Commerce Corp.	San Jose	Calif.	$40,000,000

11/21/2008	First PacTrust Bancorp, Inc.	Chula Vista	Calif.	$19,300,000
11/21/2008	Nara Bancorp, Inc.	Los Angeles	Calif.	$67,000,000
11/21/2008	Webster Financial Corporation	Waterbury	Conn.	$400,000,000
11/21/2008	Centerstate Banks of Florida Inc.	Davenport	Fla.	$27,875,000
11/21/2008	Ameris Bancorp	Moultrie	Ga.	$52,000,000
11/21/2008	Taylor Capital Group	Rosemont	Ill.	$104,823,000
11/21/2008	Porter Bancorp Inc.	Louisville	Ky.	$35,000,000
11/21/2008	Boston Private Financial Holdings, Inc.	Boston	Mass.	$154,000,000
11/21/2008	Severn Bancorp, Inc.	Annapolis	Md.	$23,393,000
11/21/2008	Trustmark Corporation	Jackson	Miss.	$215,000,000
11/21/2008	First Niagara Financial Group	Lockport	N.Y.	$184,011,000
11/21/2008	Western Alliance Bancorporation	Las Vegas	Nev.	$140,000,000
11/21/2008	First Community Corporation	Lexington	S.C.	$11,350,000
11/21/2008	HF Financial Corp.	Sioux Falls	S.D.	$25,000,000
11/21/2008	First Community Bankshares Inc.	Bluefield	Va.	$41,500,000
11/21/2008	Banner Corporation	Walla Walla	Wash.	$124,000,000
11/21/2008	Cascade Financial Corporation	Everett	Wash.	$38,970,000
11/21/2008	Columbia Banking System, Inc.	Tacoma	Wash.	$76,898,000
11/21/2008	Heritage Financial Corporation	Olympia	Wash.	$24,000,000
11/21/2008	Associated Banc-Corp	Green Bay	Wis.	$525,000,000
12/5/2008	Superior Bancorp Inc.	Birmingham	Ala.	$69,000,000
12/5/2008	Manhattan Bancorp	El Segundo	Calif.	$1,700,000
12/5/2008	East West Bancorp	Pasadena	Calif.	$306,546,000
12/5/2008	Cathay General Bancorp	Los Angeles	Calif.	$258,000,000
12/5/2008	CVB Financial Corp	Ontario	Calif.	$130,000,000
12/5/2008	Bank of Marin Bancorp	Novato	Calif.	$28,000,000
12/5/2008	Oak Valley Bancorp	Oakdale	Calif.	$13,500,000
12/5/2008	Coastal Banking Company, Inc.	Fernandina Beach	Fla.	$9,950,000
12/5/2008	TIB Financial Corp	Naples	Fla.	$37,000,000
12/5/2008	FPB Bancorp, Inc.	Port St. Lucie	Fla.	$5,800,000
12/5/2008	United Community Banks, Inc.	Blairsville	Ga.	$180,000,000
12/5/2008	MB Financial Inc.	Chicago	Ill.	$196,000,000
12/5/2008	First Midwest Bancorp, Inc.	Itasca	Ill.	$193,000,000
12/5/2008	Old National Bancorp	Evansville	Ind.	$100,000,000
12/5/2008	Blue Valley Ban Corp	Overland Park	Kan.	$21,750,000
12/5/2008	Iberiabank Corporation	Lafayette	La.	$90,000,000
12/5/2008	Central Bancorp, Inc.	Somerville	Mass.	$10,000,000
12/5/2008	Eagle Bancorp, Inc.	Bethesda	Md.	$38,235,000
12/5/2008	Sandy Spring Bancorp, Inc.	Olney	Md.	$83,094,000
12/5/2008	Old Line Bancshares, Inc.	Bowie	Md.	$7,000,000
12/5/2008	Great Southern Bancorp	Springfield	Mo.	$58,000,000
12/5/2008	Southern Missouri Bancorp, Inc.	Poplar Bluff	Mo.	$9,550,000
12/5/2008	Southern Community Financial Corp.	Winston-Salem	N.C.	$42,750,000
12/5/2008	Bank of North Carolina	Thomasville	N.C.	$31,260,000
12/5/2008	Unity Bancorp, Inc.	Clinton	N.J.	$20,649,000
12/5/2008	State Bancorp, Inc.	Jericho	N.Y.	$36,842,000
12/5/2008	First Defiance Financial Corp.	Defiance	Ohio	$37,000,000
12/5/2008	Central Federal Corporation	Fairlawn	Ohio	$7,225,000
12/5/2008	Southwest Bancorp, Inc.	Stillwater	Okla.	$70,000,000
12/5/2008	Popular, Inc.	San Juan	Puerto Rico	$935,000,000
12/5/2008	South Financial Group, Inc.	Greenville	S.C.	$347,000,000
12/5/2008	First Financial Holdings Inc.	Charleston	S.C.	$65,000,000
12/5/2008	Encore Bancshares Inc.	Houston	Texas	$34,000,000
12/5/2008	Wesbanco Bank Inc.	Wheeling	W.Va.	$75,000,000
12/5/2008	Sterling Financial Corporation	Spokane	Wash.	$303,000,000
12/12/2008	Bank Of the Ozarks Inc.	Little Rock	Ariz.	$75,000,000
12/12/2008	SVB Financial Group	Santa Clara	Calif.	$235,000,000
12/12/2008	Center Financial Corp.	Los Angeles	Calif.	$55,000,000
12/12/2008	Wilshire Bancorp Inc.	Los Angeles	Calif.	$62,158,000
12/12/2008	First Litchfield Financial Corp.	Litchfield	Conn.	$10,000,000
12/12/2008	Wilmington Trust Corp.	Wilmington	Del.	$330,000,000
12/12/2008	The Bancorp Inc.	Wilmington	Del.	$45,220,000
12/12/2008	Indiana Community Bancorp	Columbus	Ind.	$21,500,000
12/12/2008	HopFed Bancorp	Hopkinsville	Ky.	$18,400,000
12/12/2008	LSB Corp.	Andover	Mass.	$15,000,000
12/12/2008	Northeast Bancorp	Lewiston	Maine	$4,227,000
12/12/2008	Citizens Republic Bancorp Inc.	Flint	Mich.	$300,000,000
12/12/2008	Independent Bank Corp.	Ionia	Mich.	$72,000,000
12/12/2008	Capital Bank Corp.	Raliegh	N.C.	$41,279,000
12/12/2008	NewBridge Bancorp	Greensboro	N.C.	$52,372,000

12/12/2008	Citizens South Banking Corp.	Gastonia	N.C.	$20,500,000
12/12/2008	Signature Bank	New York	N.Y.	$120,000,000
12/12/2008	LNB Bancorp Inc.	Lorain	Ohio	$25,223,000
12/12/2008	Susquehanna Bancshares Inc.	Lititz	Pa.	$300,000,000
12/12/2008	National Penn Bancshares Inc.	Boyertown	Pa.	$150,000,000
12/12/2008	Fidelity Bancorp Inc.	Pittsburgh	Pa.	$7,000,000
12/12/2008	Pinnacle Financial Partners Inc.	Nashville	Tenn.	$95,000,000
12/12/2008	Sterling Bancshares Inc.	Houston	Texas	$125,198,000
12/12/2008	TowneBank	Portsmouth	Va.	$76,458,000
12/12/2008	Valley Financial Corp.	Roanoke	Va.	$16,019,000
12/12/2008	Virginia Commerce Bancorp	Arlington	Va.	$71,000,000
12/12/2008	Pacific International Bancorp	Seattle	Wash.	$6,500,000
12/19/2008	BancTrust Financial Group, Inc.	Mobile	Ala.	$50,000,000
12/19/2008	Community West Bancshares	Goleta	Calif.	$15,600,000
12/19/2008	Summit State Bank	Santa Rosa	Calif.	$8,500,000
12/19/2008	Santa Lucia Bancorp	Atascadero	Calif.	$4,000,000
12/19/2008	First California Financial Group, Inc	Westlake Village	Calif.	$25,000,000
12/19/2008	Pacific City Finacial Corporation	Los Angeles	Calif.	$16,200,000
12/19/2008	Exchange Bank	Santa Rosa	Calif.	$43,000,000
12/19/2008	NCAL Bancorp	Los Angeles	Calif.	$10,000,000
12/19/2008	CoBiz Financial Inc.	Denver	Colo.	$64,450,000
12/19/2008	The Connecticut Bank and Trust Company	Hartford	Conn.	$5,448,000
12/19/2008	Seacoast Banking Corporation of Florida	Stuart	Fla.	$50,000,000
12/19/2008	Synovus Financial Corp.	Columbus	Ga.	$967,870,000
12/19/2008	Fidelity Southern Corporation	Atlanta	Ga.	$48,200,000
12/19/2008	Heartland Financial USA, Inc.	Dubuque	Iowa	$81,698,000
12/19/2008	Intermountain Community Bancorp	Sandpoint	Idaho	$27,000,000
12/19/2008	Wintrust Financial Corporation	Lake Forest	Ill.	$250,000,000
12/19/2008	Marquette National Corporation	Chicago	Ill.	$35,500,000
12/19/2008	Bridgeview Bancorp, Inc.	Bridgeview	Ill.	$38,000,000
12/19/2008	Horizon Bancorp	Michigan City	Ind.	$25,000,000
12/19/2008	FFW Corporation	Wabash	Ind.	$7,289,000
12/19/2008	Fidelity Financial Corporation	Wichita	Kan.	$36,282,000
12/19/2008	Citizens First Corporation	Bowling Green	Ky.	$8,779,000
12/19/2008	FCB Bancorp, Inc.	Louisville	Ky.	$9,294,000
12/19/2008	Whitney Holding Corporation	New Orleans	La.	$300,000,000
12/19/2008	Wainwright Bank & Trust Company	Boston	Mass.	$22,000,000
12/19/2008	Berkshire Hills Bancorp, Inc.	Pittsfield	Mass.	$40,000,000
12/19/2008	OneUnited Bank	Boston	Mass.	$12,063,000
12/19/2008	Tri-County Financial Corporation	Waldorf	Md.	$15,540,000
12/19/2008	Patapsco Bancorp, Inc.	Dundalk	Md.	$6,000,000
12/19/2008	Enterprise Financial Services Corp.	St. Louis	Mo.	$35,000,000
12/19/2008	Hawthorn Bancshares, Inc.	Lee's Summit	Mo.	$30,255,000
12/19/2008	Monadnock Bancorp, Inc.	Peterborough	N.H.	$1,834,000
12/19/2008	Flushing Financial Corporation	Lake Success	N.Y.	$70,000,000
12/19/2008	The Elmira Savings Bank, FSB	Elmira	N.Y.	$9,090,000
12/19/2008	Alliance Financial Corporation	Syracuse	N.Y.	$26,918,000
12/19/2008	Mid Penn Bancorp, Inc.	Millersburg	Pa.	$10,000,000
12/19/2008	VIST Financial Corp.	Wyomissing	Pa.	$25,000,000
12/19/2008	AmeriServ Financial, Inc	Johnstown	Pa.	$21,000,000
12/19/2008	Bancorp Rhode Island, Inc.	Providence	R.I.	$30,000,000
12/19/2008	Security Federal Corporation	Aiken	S.C.	$18,000,000
12/19/2008	Tidelands Bancshares, Inc	Mt. Pleasant	S.C.	$14,448,000
12/19/2008	Tennessee Commerce Bancorp, Inc.	Franklin	Tenn.	$30,000,000
12/19/2008	Plains Capital Corporation	Dallas	Texas	$87,631,000
12/19/2008	Patriot Bancshares, Inc.	Houston	Texas	$26,038,000
12/19/2008	Community Bankers Trust Corporation	Glen Allen	Va.	$17,680,000
12/19/2008	Community Financial Corporation	Staunton	Va.	$12,643,000
12/19/2008	Monarch Financial Holdings, Inc.	Chesapeake	Va.	$14,700,000
12/19/2008	StellarOne Corporation	Charlottesville	Va.	$30,000,000
12/19/2008	Union Bankshares Corporation	Bowling Green	Va.	$59,000,000
12/23/2008	First Financial Bancorp	Cincinnati	Ohio	$80,000,000
12/23/2008	Bridge Capital Holdings	San Jose	Calif.	$23,864,000
12/23/2008	International Bancshares Corporation	Laredo	Texas	$216,000,000
12/23/2008	First Sound Bank	Seattle	Wash.	$7,400,000
12/23/2008	M&T Bank Corporation	Buffalo	N.Y.	$600,000,000
12/23/2008	Emclaire Financial Corp.	Emlenton	Pa.	$7,500,000
12/23/2008	Park National Corporation	Newark	Ohio	$100,000,000
12/23/2008	Green Bankshares, Inc.	Greeneville	Tenn.	$72,278,000
12/23/2008	Cecil Bancorp, Inc.	Elkton	Md.	$11,560,000

12/23/2008	Financial Institutions, Inc.	Warsaw	N.Y.	$37,515,000
12/23/2008	Fulton Financial Corporation	Lancaster	Pa.	$376,500,000
12/23/2008	United Bancorporation of Alabama, Inc.	Atmore	Ala.	$10,300,000
12/23/2008	MutualFirst Financial, Inc.	Muncie	Ind.	$32,382,000
12/23/2008	BCSB Bancorp, Inc.	Baltimore	Md.	$10,800,000
12/23/2008	HMN Financial, Inc.	Rochester	Minn.	$26,000,000
12/23/2008	First Community Bank Corporation of America	Pinellas Park	Fla.	$10,685,000
12/23/2008	Sterling Bancorp	New York	N.Y.	$42,000,000
12/23/2008	Intervest Bancshares Corporation	New York	N.Y.	$25,000,000
12/23/2008	Peoples Bancorp of North Carolina, Inc.	Newton	N.C.	$25,054,000
12/23/2008	Parkvale Financial Corporation	Monroeville	Pa.	$31,762,000
12/23/2008	Timberland Bancorp, Inc.	Hoquiam	Wash.	$16,641,000
12/23/2008	1st Constitution Bancorp	Cranbury	N.J.	$12,000,000
12/23/2008	Central Jersey Bancorp	Oakhurst	N.J.	$11,300,000
12/23/2008	Western Illinois Bancshares Inc.	Monmouth	Ill.	$6,855,000
12/23/2008	Saigon National Bank	Westminster	Calif.	$1,549,000
12/23/2008	Capital Pacific Bancorp	Portland	Ore.	$4,000,000
12/23/2008	Uwharrie Capital Corp	Albemarle	N.C.	$10,000,000
12/23/2008	Mission Valley Bancorp	Sun Valley	Calif.	$5,500,000
12/23/2008	The Little Bank, Incorporated	Kinston	N.C.	$7,500,000
12/23/2008	Pacific Commerce Bank	Los Angeles	Calif.	$4,060,000
12/23/2008	Citizens Community Bank	South Hill	Va.	$3,000,000
12/23/2008	Seacoast Commerce Bank	Chula Vista	Calif.	$1,800,000
12/23/2008	TCNB Financial Corp.	Dayton	Ohio	$2,000,000
12/23/2008	Leader Bancorp, Inc.	Arlington	Mass.	$5,830,000
12/23/2008	Nicolet Bankshares, Inc.	Green Bay	Wis.	$14,964,000
12/23/2008	Magna Bank	Memphis	Tenn.	$13,795,000
12/23/2008	Western Community Bancshares, Inc.	Palm Desert	Calif.	$7,290,000
12/23/2008	Community Investors Bancorp, Inc.	Bucyrus	Ohio	$2,600,000
12/23/2008	Capital Bancorp, Inc.	Rockville	Md.	$4,700,000
12/23/2008	Cache Valley Banking Company	Logan	Utah	$4,767,000
12/23/2008	Citizens Bancorp	Nevada City	Calif.	$10,400,000
12/23/2008	Tennessee Valley Financial Holdings, Inc.	Oak Ridge	Tenn.	$3,000,000
12/31/2008	SunTrust Banks, Inc.	Atlanta	Ga.	$1,350,000,000
12/31/2008	West Bancorporation, Inc.	West Des Moines	Iowa	$36,000,000
12/31/2008	First Banks, Inc.	Clayton	Mo.	$295,400,000
12/31/2008	CIT Group Inc.	New York	N.Y.	$2,330,000,000
12/31/2008	Fifth Third Bancorp	Cincinnati	Ohio	$3,408,000,000
12/31/2008	The PNC Financial Services Group Inc.	Pittsburgh	Pa.	$7,579,200,000
12/31/2008	Hampton Roads Bankshares, Inc.	Norfolk	Va.	$80,347,000
1/9/2009	Commerce National Bank	Newport Beach	Calif.	$5,000,000
1/9/2009	Security California Bancorp	Riverside	Calif.	$6,815,000
1/9/2009	Security Business Bancorp	San Diego	Calif.	$5,803,000
1/9/2009	Mission Community Bancorp	San Luis Obispo	Calif.	$5,116,000
1/9/2009	Valley Community Bank	Pleasanton	Calif.	$5,500,000
1/9/2009	Colony Bankcorp, Inc.	Fitzgerald	Ga.	$28,000,000
1/9/2009	The Queensborough Company	Louisville	Ga.	$12,000,000
1/9/2009	Central Pacific Financial Corp.	Honolulu	Hawaii	$135,000,000
1/9/2009	North Central Bancshares, Inc.	Fort Dodge	Iowa	$10,200,000
1/9/2009	American State Bancshares, Inc.	Great Bend	Kan.	$6,000,000
1/9/2009	Farmers Capital Bank Corporation	Frankfort	Ky.	$30,000,000
1/9/2009	First Financial Service Corporation	Elizabethtown	Ky.	$20,000,000
1/9/2009	MidSouth Bancorp, Inc.	Lafayette	La.	$20,000,000
1/9/2009	Community Trust Financial Corporation	Ruston	La.	$24,000,000
1/9/2009	Independent Bank Corp.	Rockland	Mass.	$78,158,000
1/9/2009	Shore Bancshares, Inc.	Easton	Md.	$25,000,000
1/9/2009	Rising Sun Bancorp	Rising Sun	Md.	$5,983,000
1/9/2009	The First Bancorp, Inc.	Damariscotta	Maine	$25,000,000
1/9/2009	Redwood Financial Inc.	Redwood Falls	Minn.	$2,995,000
1/9/2009	Centrue Financial Corporation	St. Louis	Mo.	$32,668,000
1/9/2009	Cadence Financial Corporation	Starkville	Miss.	$44,000,000
1/9/2009	Bank of America Corp. (Footnote 1)	Charlotte	N.C.	$10,000,000,000
1/9/2009	Crescent Financial Corporation	Cary	N.C.	$24,900,000
1/9/2009	Carolina Bank Holdings, Inc.	Greensboro	N.C.	$16,000,000
1/9/2009	First Bancorp	Troy	N.C.	$65,000,000
1/9/2009	Sound Banking Company	Morehead City	N.C.	$3,070,000
1/9/2009	Surrey Bancorp	Mount Airy	N.C.	$2,000,000
1/9/2009	Peapack-Gladstone Financial Corporation	Gladstone	N.J.	$28,685,000
1/9/2009	Sun Bancorp, Inc.	Vineland	N.J.	$89,310,000

Date	Institution	City	State	Amount
1/9/2009	Center Bancorp, Inc.	Union	N.J.	$10,000,000
1/9/2009	American Express Company	New York	N.Y.	$3,388,890,000
1/9/2009	New York Private Bank & Trust Corporation	New York	N.Y.	$267,274,000
1/9/2009	FirstMerit Corporation	Akron	Ohio	$125,000,000
1/9/2009	LCNB Corp.	Lebanon	Ohio	$13,400,000
1/9/2009	F.N.B. Corporation	Hermitage	Pa.	$100,000,000
1/9/2009	Codorus Valley Bancorp, Inc.	York	Pa.	$16,500,000
1/9/2009	Independence Bank	East Greenwich	R.I.	$1,065,000
1/9/2009	GrandSouth Bancorporation	Greenville	S.C.	$9,000,000
1/9/2009	Congaree Bancshares, Inc.	Cayce	S.C.	$3,285,000
1/9/2009	First Security Group, Inc.	Chattanooga	Tenn.	$33,000,000
1/9/2009	Texas National Bancorporation	Jacksonville	Texas	$3,981,000
1/9/2009	Eastern Virginia Bankshares, Inc.	Tappahannock	Va.	$24,000,000
1/9/2009	C&F Financial Corporation	West Point	Va.	$20,000,000
1/16/2009	Home Bancshares, Inc.	Conway	Ark	$50,000,000
1/16/2009	Southern Bancorp, Inc.	Arkadelphia	Ark.	$11,000,000
1/16/2009	Community 1st Bank	Roseville	Calif.	$2,550,000
1/16/2009	Pacific Coast National Bancorp	San Clemente	Calif.	$4,120,000
1/16/2009	Community Bank of the Bay	Oakland	Calif.	$1,747,000
1/16/2009	Redwood Capital Bancorp	Eureka	Calif.	$3,800,000
1/16/2009	Syringa Bancorp	Boise	Idaho	$8,000,000
1/16/2009	Idaho Bancorp	Boise	Idaho	$6,900,000
1/16/2009	Old Second Bancorp, Inc.	Aurora	Ill.	$73,000,000
1/16/2009	First Bankers Trustshares, Inc.	Quincy	Ill.	$10,000,000
1/16/2009	MainSource Financial Group, Inc.	Greensburg	Ind.	$57,000,000
1/16/2009	Morrill Bancshares, Inc.	Merriam	Kan.	$13,000,000
1/16/2009	Bar Harbor Bankshares/Bar Harbor Bank & Trust Bar	Harbor	Maine	$18,751,000
1/16/2009	United Bancorp, Inc.	Tecumseh	Mich.	$20,600,000
1/16/2009	Pulaski Financial Corp Creve	Coeur	Mo.	$32,538,000
1/16/2009	Dickinson Financial Corporation II	Kansas City	Mont.	$146,053,000
1/16/2009	ECB Bancorp, Inc./East Carolina Bank	Engelhard	N.C.	$17,949,000
1/16/2009	Yadkin Valley Financial Corporation	Elkin	N.C.	$36,000,000
1/16/2009	Bank of Commerce	Charlotte	N.C.	$3,000,000
1/16/2009	State Bankshares, Inc.	Fargo	N.D.	$50,000,000
1/16/2009	BNCCORP, Inc.	Bismarck	N.D.	$20,093,000
1/16/2009	New Hampshire Thrift Bancshares, Inc.	Newport	N.H.	$10,000,000
1/16/2009	Somerset Hills Bancorp	Bernardsville	N.J.	$7,414,000
1/16/2009	OceanFirst Financial Corp.	Toms River	N.J.	$38,263,000
1/16/2009	Carver Bancorp, Inc	New York	N.Y.	$18,980,000
1/16/2009	S&T Bancorp	Indiana	Pa.	$108,676,000
1/16/2009	Citizens & Northern Corporation	Wellsboro	Pa.	$26,440,000
1/16/2009	First BanCorp	San Juan	Puerto Rico	$400,000,000
1/16/2009	SCBT Financial Corporation	Columbia	S.C.	$64,779,000
1/16/2009	Texas Capital Bancshares, Inc.	Dallas	Texas	$75,000,000
1/16/2009	MetroCorp Bancshares, Inc.	Houston	Texas	$45,000,000
1/16/2009	TCB Holding Company, Texas Community Bank	The Woodlands	Texas	$11,730,000
1/16/2009	Treaty Oak Bancorp, Inc.	Austin	Texas	$3,268,000
1/16/2009	United Financial Banking Companies, Inc.	Vienna	Va.	$5,658,000
1/16/2009	Centra Financial Holdings, Inc./Centra Bank, Inc.	Morgantown	W.Va.	$15,000,000
1/16/2009	Washington Banking Company / Whidbey Island Bank	Oak Harbor	Wash.	$26,380,000
1/16/2009	Puget Sound Bank	Bellevue	Wash.	$4,500,000
1/16/2009	The Baraboo Bancorporation	Baraboo	Wis.	$20,749,000
1/16/2009	First Manitowoc Bancorp, Inc.	Manitowoc	Wis.	$12,000,000
1/22/2009	Liberty Bancshares, Inc.	Jonesboro	Ark.	$57,500,000
1/22/2009	Commonwealth Business Bank	Los Angeles	Calif.	$7,701,000
1/22/2009	CalWest Bancorp	Rancho Santa Margarita	Calif.	$4,656,000
1/22/2009	Fresno First Bank	Fresno	Calif.	$1,968,000
1/22/2009	First ULB Corp.	Oakland	Calif.	$4,900,000
1/22/2009	California Oaks State Bank	Thousand Oaks	Calif.	$3,300,000
1/22/2009	WSFS Financial Corporation	Wilmington	Del.	$52,625,000
1/22/2009	Seaside National Bank & Trust	Orlando	Fla.	$5,677,000
1/22/2009	Alarion Financial Services, Inc.	Ocala	Fla.	$6,514,000
1/22/2009	Princeton National Bancorp, Inc.	Princeton	Ill.	$25,083,000
1/22/2009	Midland States Bancorp, Inc.	Effingham	Ill.	$10,189,000

1/22/2009	Southern Illinois Bancorp, Inc.	Carmi	Ill.	$5,000,000
1/22/2009	1st Source Corporation	South Bend	Ind.	$111,000,000
1/22/2009	FPB Financial Corp.	Hammond	La.	$3,240,000
1/22/2009	Crosstown Holding Company	Blaine	Minn.	$10,650,000
1/22/2009	BankFirst Capital Corporation	Macon	Miss.	$15,500,000
1/22/2009	Calvert Financial Corporation	Ashland	Mo.	$1,037,000
1/22/2009	AB&T Financial Corporation	Gastonia	N.C.	$3,500,000
1/22/2009	First Citizens Banc Corp	Sandusky	Ohio	$23,184,000
1/22/2009	Stonebridge Financial Corp.	West Chester	Pa.	$10,973,000
1/22/2009	Moscow Bancshares, Inc.	Moscow	Tenn.	$6,216,000
1/22/2009	Farmers Bank	Windsor	Va.	$8,752,000
1/22/2009	Pierce County Bancorp	Tacoma	Wash.	$6,800,000
1/30/2009	Goldwater Bank, N.A.	Scottsdale	Ariz.	$2,568,000
1/30/2009	Rogers Bancshares, Inc.	Little Rock	Ark.	$25,000,000
1/30/2009	Peninsula Bank Holding Co.	Palo Alto	Calif.	$6,000,000
1/30/2009	Central Valley Community Bancorp	Fresno	Calif.	$7,000,000
1/30/2009	Plumas Bancorp	Quincy	Calif.	$11,949,000
1/30/2009	Valley Commerce Bancorp	Visalia	Calif.	$7,700,000
1/30/2009	Ojai Community Bank	Ojai	Calif.	$2,080,000
1/30/2009	Beach Business Bank	Manhattan Beach	Calif.	$6,000,000
1/30/2009	Bankers' Bank of tde West Bancorp, Inc.	Denver	Colo.	$12,639,000
1/30/2009	First Soutdern Bancorp, Inc.	Boca Raton	Fla.	$10,900,000
1/30/2009	Metro City Bank	Doraville	Ga.	$7,700,000
1/30/2009	PrivateBancorp, Inc.	Chicago	Ill.	$243,815,000
1/30/2009	AMB Financial Corp.	Munster	Ind.	$3,674,000
1/30/2009	UBT Bancshares, Inc.	Marysville	Kan.	$8,950,000
1/30/2009	Equity Bancshares, Inc.	Wichita	Kan.	$8,750,000
1/30/2009	Katahdin Bankshares Corp.	Houlton	Maine	$10,449,000
1/30/2009	First United Corporation	Oakland	Md.	$30,000,000
1/30/2009	Annapolis Bancorp, Inc.	Annapolis	Md.	$8,152,000
1/30/2009	Monument Bank	Betdesda	Md.	$4,734,000
1/30/2009	Flagstar Bancorp, Inc.	Troy	Mich.	$266,657,000
1/30/2009	Firstbank Corporation	Alma	Mich.	$33,000,000
1/30/2009	Guaranty Federal Bancshares, Inc.	Springfield	Mo.	$17,000,000
1/30/2009	Oak Ridge Financial Services, Inc.	Oak Ridge	N.C.	$7,700,000
1/30/2009	Nortdway Financial, Inc.	Berlin	N.H.	$10,000,000
1/30/2009	Parke Bancorp, Inc.	Sewell	N.J.	$16,288,000
1/30/2009	Stewardship Financial Corporation	Midland Park	N.J.	$10,000,000
1/30/2009	Community Partners Bancorp	Middletown	N.J.	$9,000,000
1/30/2009	Hilltop Community Bancorp, Inc.	Summit	N.J.	$4,000,000
1/30/2009	Adbanc, Inc	Ogallala	Neb.	$12,720,000
1/22/2009	Country Bank Shares, Inc.	Milford	Neb.	$7,525,000
1/22/2009	Peoples Bancorp Inc.	Marietta	Ohio	$39,000,000
1/30/2009	DNB Financial Corporation	Downingtown	Pa.	$11,750,000
1/30/2009	First Resource Bank	Exton	Pa.	$2,600,000
1/30/2009	Greer Bancshares Incorporated	Greer	S.C.	$9,993,000
1/30/2009	F & M Bancshares, Inc.	Trezevant	Tenn.	$4,609,000
1/30/2009	Central Bancshares, Inc.	Houston	Texas	$5,800,000
1/30/2009	Central Virginia Bankshares, Inc.	Powhatan	Va.	$11,385,000
1/30/2009	Middleburg Financial Corporation	Middleburg	Va.	$22,000,000
1/30/2009	WashingtonFirst Bank	Reston	Va.	$6,633,000
1/30/2009	W.T.B. Financial Corporation	Spokane	Wash.	$110,000,000
1/30/2009	Anchor BanCorp Wisconsin Inc.	Madison	Wis.	$110,000,000
1/30/2009	Legacy Bancorp, Inc.	Milwaukee	Wis.	$5,498,000
2/6/2009	Alaska Pacific Bancshares, Inc.	Juneau	Alaska	$4,781,000
2/6/2009	US Metro Bank	Garden Grove	Calif.	$2,861,000
2/6/2009	First Western Financial, Inc.	Denver	Colo.	$8,559,000
2/6/2009	Community Holding Company of Florida, Inc.	Miramar Beach	Fla.	$1,050,000
2/6/2009	Georgia Commerce Bancshares, Inc.	Atlanta	Ga.	$8,700,000
2/6/2009	PGB Holdings, Inc.	Chicago	Ill.	$3,000,000
2/6/2009	MidWestOne Financial Group, Inc.	Iowa City	Iowa	$16,000,000
2/6/2009	The Freeport State Bank	Harper	Kan.	$301,000
2/6/2009	Citizens Commerce Bancshares, Inc.	Versailles	Ky.	$6,300,000
2/6/2009	Todd Bancshares, Inc.	Hopkinsville	Ky.	$4,000,000
2/6/2009	Liberty Financial Services, Inc.	New Orleans	La.	$5,645,000
2/6/2009	Mercantile Capital Corp.	Boston	Mass.	$3,500,000
2/6/2009	Monarch Community Bancorp, Inc.	Coldwater	Mich.	$6,785,000
2/6/2009	The First Bancshares, Inc.	Hattiesburg	Miss.	$5,000,000
2/6/2009	Carolina Trust Bank	Lincolnton	N.C.	$4,000,000

2/6/2009	F & M Financial Corporation	Salisbury	N.C.	$17,000,000
2/6/2009	The Bank of Currituck	Moyock	N.C.	$4,021,000
2/6/2009	Centrix Bank & Trust	Bedford	N.H.	$7,500,000
2/6/2009	Lakeland Bancorp, Inc.	Oak Ridge	N.J.	$59,000,000
2/6/2009	Pascack Community Bank	Westwood	N.J.	$3,756,000
2/6/2009	First Express of Nebraska, Inc.	Gering	Neb.	$5,000,000
2/6/2009	Banner County Ban Corporation	Harrisburg	Neb.	$795,000
2/6/2009	Hyperion Bank	Philadelphia	Pa.	$1,552,000
2/6/2009	Stockmens Financial Corporation	Rapid City	S.D.	$15,568,000
2/6/2009	CedarStone Bank	Lebanon	Tenn.	$3,564,000
2/6/2009	Lone Star Bank	Houston	Texas	$3,072,000
2/6/2009	First Market Bank, FSB	Richmond	Va.	$33,900,000
2/6/2009	First Bank of Charleston, Inc.	Charleston	W.Va.	$3,345,000
2/13/2009	Corning Savings and Loan Association	Corning	Ark.	$638,000
2/13/2009	Westamerica Bancorporation	San Rafael	Calif.	$83,726,000
2/13/2009	1st Enterprise Bank	Los Angeles	Calif.	$4,400,000
2/13/2009	Santa Clara Valley Bank, N.A.	Santa Paula	Calif.	$2,900,000
2/13/2009	First Choice Bank	Cerritos	Calif.	$2,200,000
2/13/2009	ColoEast Bankshares, Inc.	Lamar	Colo.	$10,000,000
2/13/2009	QCR Holdings, Inc.	Moline	Ill.	$38,237,000
2/13/2009	Bern Bancshares, Inc.	Bern	Kan.	$985,000
2/13/2009	The Bank of Kentucky Financial Corporation	Crestview Hills	Ky.	$34,000,000
2/13/2009	Hometown Bancshares, Inc.	Corbin	Ky.	$1,900,000
2/13/2009	Carrollton Bancorp	Baltimore	Md.	$9,201,000
2/13/2009	State Capital Corporation	Greenwood	Miss.	$15,000,000
2/13/2009	DeSoto County Bank	Horn Lake	Miss.	$1,173,000
2/13/2009	Security Bancshares of Pulaski County, Inc.	Waynesville	Mo.	$2,152,000
2/13/2009	Reliance Bancshares, Inc.	Frontenac	Mo.	$40,000,000
2/13/2009	Gregg Bancshares, Inc.	Ozark	Mo.	$825,000
2/13/2009	Midwest Regional Bancorp, Inc.	Festus	Mo.	$700,000
2/13/2009	Liberty Bancshares, Inc.	Springfield	Mo.	$21,900,000
2/13/2009	FNB United Corp.	Asheboro	N.C.	$51,500,000
2/13/2009	PremierWest Bancorp	Medford	Ore.	$41,400,000
2/13/2009	Meridian Bank	Devon	Pa.	$6,200,000
2/13/2009	BankGreenville	Greenville	S.C.	$1,000,000
2/13/2009	Regional Bankshares, Inc.	Hartsville	S.C.	$1,500,000
2/13/2009	F&M Financial Corp.	Clarksville	Tenn.	$17,243,000
2/13/2009	Peoples Bancorp	Lynden	Wash.	$18,000,000
2/13/2009	Northwest Bancorporation, Inc.	Spokane	Wash.	$10,500,000
2/13/2009	Northwest Commercial Bank	Lakewood	Wash.	$1,992,000
2/13/2009	First Menasha Bancshares, Inc.	Neenah	Wis.	$4,797,000
2/13/2009	Financial Security Corporation	Basin	Wyo.	$5,000,000
2/20/2009	Hometown Bancorp of Alabama, Inc.	Oneonta	Ala.	$3,250,000
2/20/2009	White River Bancshares Company	Fayetteville	Ark.	$16,800,000
2/20/2009	Sonoma Valley Bancorp	Sonoma	Calif.	$8,653,000
2/20/2009	The Private Bank of California	Los Angeles	Calif.	$5,450,000
2/20/2009	United American Bank	San Mateo	Calif.	$8,700,000
2/20/2009	Premier Service Bank	Riverside	Calif.	$4,000,000
2/20/2009	Florida Business BancGroup, Inc.	Tampa	Fla.	$9,495,000
2/20/2009	Liberty Shares, Inc.	Hinesville	Ga.	$17,280,000
2/20/2009	CBB Bancorp	Cartersville	Ga.	$2,644,000
2/20/2009	Hamilton State Bancshares, Inc.	Hoschton	Ga.	$7,000,000
2/20/2009	Northern States Financial Corporation	Waukegan	Ill.	$17,211,000
2/20/2009	First BancTrust Corporation	Paris	Ill.	$7,350,000
2/20/2009	First Merchants Corporation	Muncie	Ind.	$116,000,000
2/20/2009	Market Bancorporation, Inc.	New Market	Minn.	$2,060,000
2/20/2009	Lafayette Bancorp, Inc.	Oxford	Miss.	$1,998,000
2/20/2009	BancPlus Corporation	Ridgeland	Miss.	$48,000,000
2/20/2009	Security State Bancshares, Inc.	Charleston	Mont.	$12,500,000
2/20/2009	Guaranty Bancorp, Inc.	Woodsville	N.H.	$6,920,000
2/20/2009	Royal Bancshares of Pennsylvania, Inc.	Narberth	Pa.	$30,407,000
2/20/2009	First Priority Financial Corp.	Malvern	Pa.	$4,579,000
2/20/2009	Central Community Corporation	Temple	Texas	$22,000,000
2/20/2009	Mid-Wisconsin Financial Services, Inc.	Medford	Wis.	$10,000,000
2/20/2009	Crazy Woman Creek Bancorp, Inc.	Buffalo	Wyo.	$3,100,000
2/27/2009	California Bank of Commerce	Lafayette	Calif.	$4,000,000
2/27/2009	Community Business Bank West	Sacramento	Calif.	$3,976,000
2/27/2009	FNB Bancorp South	San Francisco	Calif.	$12,000,000

2/27/2009	California Bank of Commerce	Lafayette	Calif.	$4,000,000
2/27/2009	Community Business Bank West	Sacramento	Calif.	$3,976,000
2/27/2009	FNB Bancorp South	San Francisco	Calif.	$12,000,000
2/27/2009	Columbine Capital Corp.	Buena Vista	Colo.	$2,260,000
2/27/2009	Columbine Capital Corp.	Buena Vista	Colo.	$2,260,000
2/27/2009	BNC Financial Group, Inc.	New Canaan	Conn.	$4,797,000
2/27/2009	BNC Financial Group, Inc.	New Canaan	Conn.	$4,797,000
2/27/2009	Midtown Bank & Trust Company	Atlanta	Ga.	$5,222,000
2/27/2009	Midtown Bank & Trust Company	Atlanta	Ga.	$5,222,000
2/27/2009	D.L. Evans Bancorp	Burley	Idaho	$19,891,000
2/27/2009	D.L. Evans Bancorp	Burley	Idaho	$19,891,000
2/27/2009	Lakeland Financial Corporation	Warsaw	Ind.	$56,044,000
2/27/2009	Integra Bank Corporation	Evansville	Ind.	$83,586,000
2/27/2009	Lakeland Financial Corporation	Warsaw	Ind.	$56,044,000
2/27/2009	Integra Bank Corporation	Evansville	Ind.	$83,586,000
2/27/2009	National Bancshares, Inc.	Bettendorf	Iowa	$24,664,000
2/27/2009	Green Circle Investments, Inc.	Clive	Iowa	$2,400,000
2/27/2009	National Bancshares, Inc.	Bettendorf	Iowa	$24,664,000
2/27/2009	Green Circle Investments, Inc.	Clive	Iowa	$2,400,000
2/27/2009	PSB Financial Corporation	Many	La.	$9,270,000
2/27/2009	PSB Financial Corporation	Many	La.	$9,270,000
2/27/2009	Howard Bancorp, Inc.	Ellicott City	Md.	$5,983,000
2/27/2009	Howard Bancorp, Inc.	Ellicott City	Md.	$5,983,000
2/27/2009	Private Bancorporation, Inc.	Minneapolis	Minn.	$4,960,000
2/27/2009	Private Bancorporation, Inc.	Minneapolis	Minn.	$4,960,000
2/27/2009	First M&F Corporation	Kosciusko	Miss.	$30,000,000
2/27/2009	First M&F Corporation	Kosciusko	Miss.	$30,000,000
2/27/2009	Green City Bancshares, Inc.	Green City	Mo.	$651,000
2/27/2009	Green City Bancshares, Inc.	Green City	Mo.	$651,000
2/27/2009	Catskill Hudson Bancorp, Inc	Rock Hill	N.Y.	$3,000,000
2/27/2009	Catskill Hudson Bancorp, Inc	Rock Hill	N.Y.	$3,000,000
2/27/2009	First Gothenburg Bancshares, Inc.	Gothenburg	Neb.	$7,570,000
2/27/2009	First Gothenburg Bancshares, Inc.	Gothenburg	Neb.	$7,570,000
2/27/2009	Regent Capital Corporation	Nowata	Okla.	$2,655,000
2/27/2009	Regent Capital Corporation	Nowata	Okla.	$2,655,000
2/27/2009	TriState Capital Holdings, Inc.	Pittsburgh	Pa.	$23,000,000
2/27/2009	The Victory Bank	Limerick	Pa.	$541,000
2/27/2009	TriState Capital Holdings, Inc.	Pittsburgh	Pa.	$23,000,000
2/27/2009	The Victory Bank	Limerick	Pa.	$541,000
2/27/2009	Southern First Bancshares, Inc.	Greenville	S.C.	$17,299,000
2/27/2009	Southern First Bancshares, Inc.	Greenville	S.C.	$17,299,000
2/27/2009	Community First Inc.	Columbia	Tenn.	$17,806,000
2/27/2009	Avenue Financial Holdings, Inc.	Nashville	Tenn.	$7,400,000
2/27/2009	Community First Inc.	Columbia	Tenn.	$17,806,000
2/27/2009	Avenue Financial Holdings, Inc.	Nashville	Tenn.	$7,400,000
2/27/2009	First State Bank of Mobeetie	Mobeetie	Texas	$731,000
2/27/2009	Central Bancorp, Inc.	Garland	Texas	$22,500,000
2/27/2009	First State Bank of Mobeetie	Mobeetie	Texas	$731,000
2/27/2009	Central Bancorp, Inc.	Garland	Texas	$22,500,000
2/27/2009	Medallion Bank	Salt Lake City	Utah	$11,800,000
2/27/2009	Medallion Bank	Salt Lake City	Utah	$11,800,000
2/27/2009	Ridgestone Financial Services, Inc.	Brookfield	Wis.	$10,900,000
2/27/2009	Ridgestone Financial Services, Inc.	Brookfield	Wis.	$10,900,000
3/6/2009	First Federal Bancshares of Arkansas, Inc.	Harrison	Ark.	$16,500,000
3/6/2009	ICB Financial	Ontario	Calif.	$6,000,000
3/6/2009	First Southwest Bancorporation, Inc.	Alamosa	Colo.	$5,500,000
3/6/2009	Highlands Independent Bancshares, Inc.	Sebring	Fla.	$6,700,000
3/6/2009	Pinnacle Bank Holding Company, Inc.	Orange City	Fla.	$4,389,000
3/6/2009	Marine Bank & Trust Company	Vero Beach	Fla.	$3,000,000
3/6/2009	Regent Bancorp, Inc.	Davie	Fla.	$9,982,000
3/6/2009	Citizens Bancshares Corporation	Atlanta	Ga.	$7,462,000
3/6/2009	PeoplesSouth Bancshares, Inc.	Colquitt	Ga.	$12,325,000
3/6/2009	First Busey Corporation	Urbana	Ill.	$100,000,000
3/6/2009	Blue River Bancshares, Inc.	Shelbyville	Ind.	$5,000,000
3/6/2009	Community Bancshares of Kansas, Inc.	Goff	Kan.	$500,000
3/6/2009	Blue Ridge Bancshares, Inc.	Independence	Mo.	$12,000,000
3/6/2009	AmeriBank Holding Company	Collinsville	Okla.	$2,492,000
3/6/2009	HCSB Financial Corporation	Loris	S.C.	$12,895,000
3/6/2009	First Reliance Bancshares, Inc.	Florence	S.C.	$15,349,000
3/6/2009	Merchants and Planters Bancshares, Inc.	Toone	Tenn.	$1,881,000

Date	Institution	City	State	Amount
3/6/2009	Germantown Capital Corporation, Inc.	Germantown	Tenn.	$4,967,000
3/6/2009	First Texas BHC, Inc.	Fort Worth	Texas	$13,533,000
3/6/2009	Farmers & Merchants Bancshares, Inc.	Houston	Texas	$11,000,000
3/6/2009	BOH Holdings, Inc.	Houston	Texas	$10,000,000
3/6/2009	Park Bancorporation, Inc.	Madison	Wis.	$23,200,000
3/13/2009	BancIndependent, Inc.	Sheffield	Ala.	$21,100,000
3/13/2009	First Northern Community Bancorp	Dixon	Calif.	$17,390,000
3/13/2009	Salisbury Bancorp, Inc.	Lakeville	Conn.	$8,816,000
3/13/2009	1st United Bancorp, Inc.	Boca Raton	Fla.	$10,000,000
3/13/2009	First Intercontinental Bank	Doraville	Ga.	$6,398,000
3/13/2009	Discover Financial Services	Riverwoods	Ill.	$1,224,558,000
3/13/2009	Butler Point, Inc.	Catlin	Ill.	$607,000
3/13/2009	Haviland Bancshares, Inc.	Haviland	Kan.	$425,000
3/13/2009	Madison Financial Corporation	Richmond	Ky.	$3,370,000
3/13/2009	St. Johns Bancshares, Inc.	St. Louis	Mo.	$3,000,000
3/13/2009	First American International Corp.	Brooklyn	N.Y.	$17,000,000
3/13/2009	IBW Financial Corporation	Washington DC	n/a	$6,000,000
3/13/2009	Bank of George	Las Vegas	Nev.	$2,672,000
3/13/2009	First Place Financial Corp.	Warren	Ohio	$72,927,000
3/13/2009	Provident Community Bancshares, Inc.	Rock Hill	S.C.	$9,266,000
3/13/2009	Moneytree Corporation	Lenoir City	Tenn.	$9,516,000
3/13/2009	Sovereign Bancshares, Inc.	Dallas	Texas	$18,215,000
3/13/2009	First National Corporation	Strasburg	Va.	$13,900,000
3/13/2009	Blackhawk Bancorp, Inc.	Beloit	Wis.	$10,000,000
3/20/2009	Heritage Oaks Bancorp	Paso Robles	Calif.	$21,000,000
3/20/2009	Premier Bank Holding Company	Tallahassee	Fla.	$9,500,000
3/20/2009	Farmers & Merchants Financial Corporation	Argonia	Kan.	$442,000
3/20/2009	Farmers State Bankshares, Inc.	Holton	Kan.	$700,000
3/20/2009	First NBC Bank Holding Company	New Orleans	La.	$17,836,000
3/20/2009	Citizens Bank & Trust Company	Covington	La.	$2,400,000
3/20/2009	Kirksville Bancorp, Inc.	Kirksville	Mo.	$470,000
3/20/2009	First Colebrook Bancorp, Inc.	Colebrook	N.H.	$4,500,000
3/20/2009	Community First Bancshares Inc.	Union City	Tenn.	$20,000,000
3/20/2009	Peoples Bancshares of TN, Inc.	Madisonville	Tenn.	$3,900,000
3/27/2009	SBT Bancorp, Inc.	Simsbury	Conn.	$4,000,000
3/27/2009	CSRA Bank Corp.	Wrens	Ga.	$2,400,000
3/27/2009	Trinity Capital Corporation	Los Alamos	N.M.	$35,539,000
3/27/2009	Clover Community Bankshares, Inc.	Clover	S.C.	$3,000,000
3/27/2009	Pathway Bancorp	Cairo	Neb.	$3,727,000
3/27/2009	Colonial American Bank West	Conshohocken	Pa.	$574,000
3/27/2009	MS Financial, Inc.	Kingwood	Texas	$7,723,000
3/27/2009	Triad Bancorp, Inc.	Frontenac	Mo.	$3,700,000
3/27/2009	Alpine Banks of Colorado	Glenwood Springs	Colo.	$70,000,000
3/27/2009	Naples Bancorp, Inc.	Naples	Fla.	$4,000,000
3/27/2009	CBS Banc-Corp.	Russellville	Ala.	$24,300,000
3/27/2009	IBT Bancorp, Inc.	Irving	Texas	$2,295,000
3/27/2009	Spirit BankCorp, Inc.	Bristow	Okla.	$30,000,000
3/27/2009	Maryland Financial Bank	Towson	Md.	$1,700,000
4/3/2009	First Capital Bancorp, Inc.	Glen Ellen	Va.	$10,958,000
4/3/2009	Tri-State Bank of Memphis	Memphis	Tenn.	$2,795,000
4/3/2009	Fortune Financial Corporation	Arnold	Mo.	$3,100,000
4/3/2009	BancStar, Inc.	Festus	Mo.	$8,600,000
4/3/2009	Titonka Bancshares, Inc	Titonka	Iowa	$2,117,000
4/3/2009	Millennium Bancorp, Inc.	Edwards	Colo.	$7,260,000
4/3/2009	TriSummit Bank	Kingsport	Tenn.	$2,765,000
4/3/2009	Prairie Star Bancshares, Inc.	Olathe	Kan.	$2,800,000
4/3/2009	Community First Bancshares, Inc.	Harrison	Ark.	$12,725,000
4/3/2009	BCB Holding Company, Inc.	Theodore	Ala.	$1,706,000
4/10/2009	City National Bancshares Corporation	Newark	N.J.	$9,439,000
4/10/2009	First Business Bank, N.A.	San Diego	Calif.	$2,211,000
4/10/2009	SV Financial, Inc.	Sterling	Ill.	$4,000,000
4/10/2009	Capital Commerce Bancorp, Inc.	Milwaukee	Wis.	$5,100,000
4/10/2009	Metropolitan Capital Bancorp, Inc.	Chicago	Ill.	$2,040,000
4/17/2009	Bank of the Carolinas Corporation	Mocksville	N.C.	$13,179,000
4/17/2009	Penn Liberty Financial Corp.	Wayne	Pa.	$9,960,000
4/17/2009	Tifton Banking Company	Tifton	Ga.	$3,800,000
4/17/2009	Patterson Bancshares, Inc	Patterson	La.	$3,690,000
4/17/2009	BNB Financial Services Corporation	New York	N.Y.	$7,500,000
4/17/2009	Omega Capital Corp.	Lakewood	Colo.	$2,816,000

4/24/2009	Mackinac Financial Corporation / mBank	Manistique	Mich.	$11,000,000
4/24/2009	Birmingham Bloomfield Bancshares, Inc	Birmingham	Mich.	$1,635,000
4/24/2009	Vision Bank - Texas	Richardson	Texas	$1,500,000
4/24/2009	Oregon Bancorp, Inc.	Salem	Ore.	$3,216,000
4/24/2009	Peoples Bancorporation, Inc.	Easley	S.C.	$12,660,000
4/24/2009	Indiana Bank Corp.	Dana	Ind.	$1,312,000
4/24/2009	Business Bancshares, Inc.	Clayton	Mo.	$15,000,000
4/24/2009	Standard Bancshares, Inc.	Hickory Hills	Ill.	$60,000,000
4/24/2009	York Traditions Bank	York	Pa.	$4,871,000
4/24/2009	Grand Capital Corporation	Tulsa	Okla.	$4,000,000
4/24/2009	Allied First Bancorp, Inc.	Oswego	Ill.	$3,652,000
4/24/2009	Frontier Bancshares, Inc.	Austin	Texas	$3,000,000
5/1/2009	Village Bank and Trust Financial Corp.	Midlothian	Va.	$14,738,000
5/1/2009	CenterBank	Milford	Ohio	$2,250,000
5/1/2009	Georgia Primary Bank	Atlanta	Ga.	$4,500,000
5/1/2009	Union Bank & Trust Company	Oxford	N.C.	$3,194,000
5/1/2009	HPK Financial Corporation	Chicago	Ill.	$4,000,000
5/1/2009	OSB Financial Services, Inc.	Orange	Texas	$6,100,000
5/1/2009	Security State Bank Holding-Company	Jamestown	N.D.	$10,750,000
5/8/2009	Highlands State Bank	Vernon	N.J.	$3,091,000
5/8/2009	One Georgia Bank	Atlanta	Ga.	$5,500,000
5/8/2009	Gateway Bancshares, Inc.	Ringgold	Ga.	$6,000,000
5/8/2009	Freeport Bancshares, Inc.	Freeport	Ill.	$3,000,000
5/8/2009	Investors Financial Corporation of Pettis County, Inc.	Sedalia	Mo.	$4,000,000
5/8/2009	Sword Financial Corporation	Horicon	Wis.	$13,644,000
5/8/2009	Premier Bancorp, Inc.	Wilmette	Ill.	$6,784,000
5/15/2009	Mercantile Bank Corporation	Grand Rapids	Mich.	$21,000,000
5/15/2009	Northern State Bank	Closter	N.J.	$1,341,000
5/15/2009	Western Reserve Bancorp, Inc	Medina	Ohio	$4,700,000
5/15/2009	Community Financial Shares, Inc.	Glen Ellyn	Ill.	$6,970,000
5/15/2009	Worthington Financial Holdings, Inc.	Huntsville	Ala.	$2,720,000
5/15/2009	First Community Bancshares, Inc	Overland Park	Kan.	$14,800,000
5/15/2009	Southern Heritage Bancshares, Inc.	Cleveland	Tenn.	$4,862,000
5/15/2009	Foresight Financial Group, Inc.	Rockford	Ill.	$15,000,000
5/15/2009	IBC Bancorp, Inc.	Chicago	Ill.	$4,205,000
5/15/2009	Boscobel Bancorp, Inc	Boscobel	Wis.	$5,586,000
5/15/2009	Brogan Bankshares, Inc.	Kaukauna	Wis.	$2,400,000
5/15/2009	Riverside Bancshares, Inc.	Little Rock	Ark.	$1,100,000
5/15/2009	Deerfield Financial Corporation	Deerfield	Wis.	$2,639,000
5/15/2009	Market Street Bancshares, Inc.	Mt. Vernon	Ill.	$20,300,000
5/22/2009	The Landrum Company	Columbia	Mo..	$15,000,000
5/22/2009	First Advantage Bancshares Inc.	Coon Rapids	Minn.	$1,177,000
5/22/2009	Fort Lee Federal Savings Bank	Fort Lee	N.J.	$1,300,000
5/22/2009	Blackridge Financial, Inc.	Fargo	N.D.	$5,000,000
5/22/2009	Illinois State Bancorp, Inc.	Chicago	Ill.	$6,272,000
5/22/2009	Universal Bancorp	Bloomfield	Ind.	$9,900,000
5/22/2009	Franklin Bancorp, Inc.	Washington	Mo.	$5,097,000
5/22/2009	Commonwealth Bancshares, Inc.	Louisville	Ky.	$20,400,000
5/22/2009	Premier Financial Corp	Dubuque	Iowa	$6,349,000
5/22/2009	F & C Bancorp, Inc.	Holden	Mo.	$2,993,000
5/22/2009	Diamond Bancorp, Inc.	Washington	Mo.	$20,445,000
5/22/2009	United Bank Corporation	Barnesville	Ga.	$14,400,000
5/29/2009	Community Bank Shares of Indiana, Inc.	New Albany	Ind.	$19,468,000
5/29/2009	American Premier Bancorp	Arcadia	Calif.	$1,800,000
5/29/2009	CB Holding Corp.	Aledo	Ill.	$4,114,000
5/29/2009	Citizens Bancshares Co.	Chillicothe	Mo.	$24,990,000
5/29/2009	Grand Mountain Bancshares, Inc.	Granby	Colo.	$3,076,000
5/29/2009	Two Rivers Financial Group	Burlington	Iowa	$12,000,000
5/29/2009	Fidelity Bancorp, Inc	Baton Rouge	La.	$3,942,000
5/29/2009	Chambers Bancshares, Inc.	Danville	Ark.	$19,817,000
6/5/2009	Covenant Financial Corporation	Clarksdale	Miss.	$5,000,000
6/5/2009	First Trust Corporation	New Orleans	La.	$17,969,000
6/5/2009	OneFinancial Corporation	Little Rock	Ark.	$17,300,000
6/12/2009	Berkshire Bancorp, Inc.	Wyomissing	Pa.	$2,892,000
6/12/2009	First Vernon Bancshares, Inc.	Vernon	Ala.	$6,000,000
6/12/2009	SouthFirst Bancshares, Inc.	Sylacauga	Ala.	$2,760,000
6/12/2009	Virginia Company Bank	Newport News	Va.	$4,700,000
6/12/2009	Enterprise Financial Services Group, Inc.	Allison Park	Pa.	$4,000,000
6/12/2009	First Financial Bancshares, Inc.	Lawrence	Kan.	$3,756,000

Date	Company	City	State	Amount
6/12/2009	River Valley Bancorporation, Inc.	Wausau	Wis.	$15,000,000
6/12/2009	Berkshire Bancorp, Inc.	Wyomissing	Pa.	$2,892,000
6/12/2009	First Vernon Bancshares, Inc.	Vernon	Ala.	$6,000,000
6/12/2009	SouthFirst Bancshares, Inc.	Sylacauga	Ala.	$2,760,000
6/12/2009	Virginia Company Bank	Newport News	Va.	$4,700,000
6/12/2009	Enterprise Financial Services Group, Inc.	Allison Park	Pa.	$4,000,000
6/12/2009	First Financial Bancshares, Inc.	Lawrence	Kan.	$3,756,000
6/12/2009	River Valley Bancorporation, Inc.	Wausau	Wis.	$15,000,000
6/19/2009	Merchants and Manufacturers Bank Corporation	Joliet	Ill.	$3,510,000
6/19/2009	RCB Financial Corporation	Rome	Ga.	$8,900,000
6/19/2009	Manhattan Bancshares, Inc.	Manhattan	Ill.	$2,639,000
6/19/2009	Biscayne Bancshares, Inc.	Coconut Grove	Fla.	$6,400,000
6/19/2009	Duke Financial Group, Inc.	Minneapolis	Minn.	$12,000,000
6/19/2009	Farmers Enterprises, Inc.	Great Bend	Kan.	$12,000,000
6/19/2009	Century Financial Services Corporation	Santa Fe	N.M.	$10,000,000
6/19/2009	NEMO Bancshares Inc.	Madison	Mo.	$2,330,000
6/19/2009	University Financial Corp, Inc.	St. Paul	Minn.	$11,926,000
6/19/2009	Suburban Illinois Bancorp, Inc.	Elmhurst	Ill.	$15,000,000
6/26/2009	Hartford Financial Services Group, Inc.	Hartford	Conn.	$3,400,000,000
6/26/2009	Fidelity Resources Company	Plano	Texas	$3,000,000
6/26/2009	Waukesha Bankshares, Inc.	Waukesha	Wis.	$5,625,000
6/26/2009	FC Holdings, Inc.	Houston	Texas	$21,042,000
6/26/2009	Security Capital Corporation	Batesville	Miss.	$17,388,000
6/26/2009	First Alliance Bancshares, Inc.	Cordova	Tenn.	$3,422,000
6/26/2009	Gulfstream Bancshares, Inc.	Stuart	Fla.	$7,500,000
6/26/2009	Gold Canyon Bank Gold	Canyon	Ariz.	$1,607,000
6/26/2009	M&F Bancorp, Inc.	Durham	N.C.	$11,735,000
6/26/2009	Metropolitan Bank Group, Inc.	Chicago	Ill.	$71,526,000
6/26/2009	NC Bancorp, Inc.	Chicago	Ill.	$6,880,000
6/26/2009	Alliance Bancshares, Inc.	Dalton	Ga.	$2,986,000
6/26/2009	Stearns Financial Services, Inc.	St. Cloud	Minn.	$24,900,000
6/26/2009	Signature Bancshares, Inc.	Dallas	Texas	$1,700,000
6/26/2009	Fremont Bancorporation	Fremont	Calif.	$35,000,000
6/26/2009	Alliance Financial Services Inc.	St. Paul	Minn.	$12,000,000
7/10/2009	Lincoln National Corporation	Radnor	Pa.	$950,000,000
7/10/2009	Bancorp Financial, Inc.	Oak Brook	Ill.	$13,669,000
7/17/2009	Brotherhood Bancshares, Inc.	Kansas City	Kan.	$11,000,000
7/17/2009	SouthCrest Financial Group, Inc.	Fayetteville	Ga.	$12,900,000
7/17/2009	Harbor Bankshares Corporation	Baltimore	Md.	$6,800,000
7/17/2009	First South Bancorp, Inc.	Lexington	Tenn.	$50,000,000
7/17/2009	Great River Holding Company	Baxter	Minn.	$8,400,000
7/17/2009	Plato Holdings Inc.	St. Paul	Minn.	$2,500,000
7/24/2009	Yadkin Valley Financial Corp.	Elkin	N.C.	$13,312,000
7/24/2009	Community Bancshares, Inc.	Kingman	Ariz.	$3,872,000
7/24/2009	Florida Bank Group, Inc.	Tampa	Fla.	$20,471,000
7/24/2009	First American Bank Corp.	Elk Grove Village	Ill.	$50,000,000
7/31/2009	Chicago Shore Corp.	Chicago	Ill.	$7,000,000
7/31/2009	Financial Services of Winger, Inc.	Winger	Minn.	$3,742,000
8/7/2009	The ANB Corporation	Terrell	Texas	$20,000,000
8/7/2009	U.S. Century Bank	Miami	Fla.	$50,236,000
8/14/2009	Bank Financial Services, Inc.	Eden Prarie	Minn.	$1,004,000
8/21/2009	KS Bancorp Inc.	Smithfield	N.C.	$4,000,000
8/21/2009	AmFirst Financial Services Inc.	McCook	Neb.	$5,000,000
8/28/2009	First Independence Corp.	Detroit	Mich.	$3,223,000
8/28/2009	First Guaranty Bancshares Inc.	Hammond	La.	$20,699,000
8/28/2009	CoastalSouth Bancshares Inc.	Hilton Head Island	S.C.	$16,015,000
8/28/2009	TCB Corporation	Greenwood	S.C.	$9,720,000
9/4/2009	The State Bank of Bartley	Bartley	Neb.	$1,697,000
9/11/2009	Pathfinder Bancorp, Inc.	Oswego	N.Y.	$6,771,000
9/11/2009	Community Bancshares of Mississippi, Inc.	Brandon	Miss.	$52,000,000
9/11/2009	Heartland Bancshares, Inc.	Franklin	Ind.	$7,000,000
9/11/2009	PFSB Bancorporation, Inc.	Pigeon Falls	Wis.	$1,500,000
9/11/2009	First Eagle Bancshares, Inc.	Hanover Park	Ill.	$7,500,000
9/18/2009	IA Bancorp, Inc.	Iselin	N.J.	$5,976,000
9/18/2009	HomeTown Bankshares Corporation	Roanoke	Va.	$10,000,000
9/25/2009	Heritage Bankshares Inc.	Norfolk	Va.	$10,103,000
9/25/2009	Mountain Valley Bancshares	Cleveland	Ga.	$3,300,000
9/25/2009	Grand Financial Corp.	Hattiesburg	Miss.	$2,443,320
9/25/2009	Guaranty Capital Corp.	Belzoni	Miss.	$14,000,000

9/25/2009	GulfSouth Private Bank	Destin	Fla.	$7,500,000
9/25/2009	Steele Street Bank Corp.	Denver	Colo.	$11,019,000
10/2/2009	Premier Financial Bancorp	Huntington	W.Va.	$22,252,000
10/2/2009	Providence Bank	Rocky Mount	N.C.	$4,000,000
10/23/2009	Regents Bancshares	Vancouver	Wash.	$12,700,000
10/23/2009	Cardinal Bancorp II	Washington	Mo.	$6,251,000
10/30/2009	Randolph Bank & Trust Co.	Asheboro	N.C..	$6,229,000
10/30/2009	WashingtonFirst Bankshares	Reston	Va.	$6,842,000
11/6/2009	F & M Bancshares	Trezevant	Tenn.	$3,535,000
11/20/2009	**Presidio Bank**	San Francisco	Calif.	$10,800,000
11/20/2009	**McLeod Bancshares**	Shorewood	Minn.	$6,000,000
11/20/2009	**Metropolitan Capital Bancorp**	Chicago	Ill.	$2,348,000
12/4/2009	**Broadway Financial Corp.**	Los Angeles	Calif.	$6,000,000
12/04/09	**Delmar Bancorp**	Delmar	Md.	$9,000,000
12/4/2009	**Liberty Bancshares**	Fort Worth	Texas	$6,500,000

Shocked by that list? I put it there for you to use as a future reference, and for a little wake up call. I know it is long but it is useful. Is your cash on one of these banks? If so consider the solvency of your institution.

There is more. That list includes a total of just under $205 Billion, however the total bailout under TARP (Troubled Asset Relief Program) was supposed to be 700 Billion. So where did the rest of it go? The Treasury now owns stock in hundreds of banks as well as companies such as, General Motors, Chrysler, A.I.G., Bank of America, Citigroup, Freddie Mac, and Fannie Mae.

What must also be understood is this: each entity which received bailouts has now become a further servant of the central banks which are again privately owned entities, and the world's central banks are owned, managed, controlled, and overseen by Wall Street.

Wall Street Rules The World...

Not Presidents, Senators, Representatives, Kings, Queens, Monarchs, Dictators, etc. etc.

This is a quote I would like you to consider;

"Give me control over a nations currency and I care not who makes it's laws"

B. Rothschild.

The simple fact is this: the global financial system which is all under control by the same entities has become a twisted scheme which is run by the few in what has been a very successful scheme to control and fleece the many.

Section 7

What Is The Business Of World Governments?

I am an American citizen and I believe in what our Forefathers sacrificed so much in order to accomplish. Our Forefathers envisioned a system of government in which ALL would share in great prosperity while building the greatest nation the world had ever seen. A system in which not just the few, but everyone would be able to reap what he/she had sown.

This is the Preamble to the United States Constitution:

We the People of the United States, in order to form a more perfect union, establish justice, insure domestic tranquility, provide for the common defense, promote the general welfare, and secure the blessings of liberty to ourselves and our posterity, do ordain and establish this constitution for the United States of America. Our Forefathers established that only Gold and Silver be used as payment of debts: here is a quote from Article 1 Section 10 of the U.S. Constitution *"No State shall make anything but gold and silver coin a tender in payment of debts"*

Let us first elaborate on the Preamble to the U.S. Constitution: from the very first words of this living document it was established that this new fledgeling nation was to be one created *by and for the people.* Furthermore, Article 1 Section 10 establishes that no monetary system other than that which is backed by gold and silver be used in ANY WAY. These two aspects of the United States Constitution are in fact the cornerstones of the entire idea put forth by our Forefathers, and they were very aware that without them the entire system as a whole would be vulnerable to gross perversion and manipulation..and this is precisely what has happened, a grim reality that you and I face at this very moment.

The idea of a free and capitalistic society is the driving force behind the establishment of a true democratic system. An economic model in which the fair market value of a given asset is determined by a free market and a sound money system is the framework which our Forefathers wanted, however this is in no way the system which is in place today. Subsequently this abomination exists not just here in the United States, but every single other modern economic system in the world today and this did not happen by accident.

Fascism defined: a corporate state controlled by the government. In section 1 of this book I established the fact that the government is in bed with the entire financial system. This system is run by the central banks and Wall Street. The current system here in America is Fascism defined. As we know, in 1971 here in the United States we were stripped of our gold standard (a deviation from the vision of our Forefathers who expressly wanted a sound money system based upon gold and silver). Subsequently two years after losing our gold standard the petrodollar system was created. This vaulted the U.S. Dollar to global reserve status and it has held that position since that time. With the implementation of the now fiat monetary system and the petrodollar, the central bankers could now simply print cash out of thin air, distribute, and charge interest on that fake money. Subsequently this system would create wealth for central bankers beyond imagination. With the currency being printed and backed by nothing, the central banks succeeded in creating a nation of slaves. Actually a world of slaves, because every other modern economic model is also based upon a fiat system and the U.S. Dollar is still the world reserve currency. People are willing to work for these pieces of paper with numbers printed on them which have no actual value because they believe that they represent actual wealth, they do not. It is just an illusion. Each bill you hold is debt, it is just a promissory note which is owned and owed back to the central bank which issued it plus any interest it will accrue.

We have discussed how the economies of the United States as well as every other fiat founded economic model is based upon the accumulation of debt in perpetuity, a system which is unsustainable. At the point when no more debt can be accrued a crisis ensues just like we are witnessing in Europe, and what is the solution from the policy makers? Add on even more debt with bailouts for banks, corporations, other institutions, using public funds and then force austerity on the public. Austerity chokes economic growth which in turn generates less tax revenue. So we realize that the issue is debt, meanwhile more debt is continually being added. How can a slowing economy being pushed even slower by austerity possibly pay back not just the debt issue which was the initial problem, but the more debt being added? It simply cannot be done and a much greater global financial catastrophe is looming.

It would seem logical the the business of government would be in the best interests of its citizens, and this model is the one envisioned by the designers of the Constitution here in the United States. This should also be the system followed by any governing body in again, a free and democratic society, however it is no longer the case. Globally as we have already established, the entire system has become perverted into a scheme which benefits the few over the many, in fact the very few. We now know these few entities as the politicocorporatists. The politicocorporatists are comprised of three groups and they are: 1. The policymakers, 2. The central banks, and 3. The corporate insiders. These three components coincidentally make up the military industrial complex. The ultimate goal of the military industrial complex is to establish, dominate, and control every aspect of human endeavor on a world wide scale. They use war as a mechanism to generate enormous wealth for themselves.

Their lust for wealth through the gamy of war, under the guise of necessity brought about by the propagation of fear, is done without prejudice. In the wake of their unrelenting pursuit of over abundance is the blood and guts of countless millions soldiers and civilians alike, along with destroyed lives and misery for most others involved in direct conflict. No other "civilized" nation has been involved in more military campaigns, both large and small, than the United States. This is not just mere coincidence either. Keep in mind that many of the world's largest corporations would not exist if it were not for the propagation of the war machine. Here is a list of corporations directly involved with and who have a vested interest in the constant expansion of war.

Below is a list of corporations involved in weapons manufacturing listed by name in alphabetical order and country.

Accuracy International	UK
Air Weapons Complex (AWC)	Pakistan
Alexander Arms	USA
Antonov	Ukraine
Alliant Techsystems	USA
Arcus Co.	Bulgaria
Aquarius International	PAK
Aquarius International	AUS
Aquarius International	SG
ArmaLite	USA
Armi Jager	Italy
Armament Technology	Canada
Armscor	Philippines
Arsenal Corporation	Bulgaria
Arsenal, Inc.	USA
Astra Arms	Switzerland
Kiev Arsenal	Ukraine
ASELSAN	Turkey
Atlas Elektronik	Germany
Avibras	Brazil

BAE Systems	UK
BAE Systems AB	Sweden
Baikal	Russia
Bangladesh Ordnance Factories	Bangladesh
Barrett Firearms Manufacturing	USA
Bazalt	Russia
Benelli	Italy
Beretta	Italy
Bharat Dynamics	India
Bharat Earth Movers Limited	India
Bharat Electronics Limited	India
Birmingham Small Arms Company	UK
Boeing Defense, Space & Security	USA
Browning Arms Company	Belgium
Bushmaster Firearms International	USA
Caspian Arms Ltd	USA
Chaiseri Metal & Rubber	Thailand
Charles Daly	USA
Charter Arms	USA
CheyTac	USA
Colt Canada (formerly Diemaco)	Canada
Colt's Manufacturing Company (CMC)	USA
Companhia Brasileira de Cartuchos (CBC)	Brazil
Česká Zbrojovka Strakonice	Czech Republic
Česká Zbrojovka Uherský Brod	Czech Republic
Defense Industries Organization	Iran
Degtyarev Plant	Russia
Denel	South Africa
Denel Dynamics	South Africa
Detonics	USA
Diehl BGT Defence	Germany
Doosan DST	South Korea
EADS	Europe
EAS	Greece
Elbit Systems	Israel
Embraer	Brazil
Fábrica de Armas Halcón	Argentina

Fabrique Nationale (FN)	Belgium
Fabryka Broni "Łucznik" - Radom	Poland
FAMAE	Chile
FAMARS	Italy
Federal Cartridge Company	USA
Fegyver- és Gépgyár (FEG)	Hungary
Ferfrans	Philippines
Finmeccanica	Italy
Floro International Corporation	Philippines
General Dynamics	USA
Nexter (formerly GIAT Industries)	France
Glock Ges.m.b.H.	Austria
Grand Power	Slovakia
Hanwha	South Korea
Heavy Industries Taxila	Pakistan
Heckler & Koch (H&K)	Germany
Henry Repeating Arms	USA
Hispano Argentina Fábrica de Automóviles	Argentina
Helibras	Brazil
Hi-Point Firearms	USA
Hindustan Aeronautics Limited	India
Holland & Holland	UK
Howaldtswerke-Deutsche Werft (HDW)	Germany
HS Produkt	Croatia
Hyundai Rotem	South Korea
IBRAP	Brazil
Iran Aviation Industries Organization	Iran
Iran Electronics Industries	Iran
IMBEL	Brazil
INDEP	Portugal
Indumil	Colombia
Innalabs	Ireland
Insys	UK
Israel Military Industries (IMI)	Israel
Israel Weapon Industries (IWI)	Israel
Israel Aerospace Industries (IAI)	Israel
Izhevsk Mechanical Plant	Russia

Izhmash	Russia
James Purdey and Sons Ltd.	UK
JP Enterprises Inc	USA
Kahr Arms	USA
KBP Instrument Design Bureau	Russia
Kel-Tec CNC Industries Inc	USA
Kharkiv Morozov Machine Building Design Bureau	Ukraine
Kimber Manufacturing	USA
Klimovsk Specialized Ammunition Plant	Russia
Knight's Armament Company (KAC)	USA
Kongsberg Defence & Aerospace	Norway
Korea Aerospace Industries (KAI)	South Korea
KAL-ASD	South Korea
Krauss-Maffei Wegmann (KMW)	Germany
Land Warfare Resources Corporation (LWRC)	USA
Les Baer	USA
LFK	Germany
LIG nex1	South Korea
Lockheed Martin	USA
Franchi	Italy
Lürssen	Germany
Magnum Research Inc. (MRI)	USA
Mechanical and Chemical Industry Corporation (MKEK)	Turkey
Manroy Engineering Ltd.	UK
Manroy USA	USA
MasterPiece Arms	USA
Mauser	Germany
Marlin Firearms	USA
Matra BAE Dynamics Alenia (MBDA)	France
McBros Rifles	USA
Miguel Enrique Manzo Sal (MEMS)	Argentina
Metal Storm	Australia
Malyshev Factory	Ukraine
Nammo	Norway
Norinco	China
Northrop Corporation	USA
O.F. Mossberg & Sons	USA

Oerlikon Contraves	Switzerland
Olympic Arms	USA
OMI Ordtech Military Industries	Greece
Ordnance Factories Board	India
Pakistan Aeronautical Complex (PAC)	Pakistan
Pakistan Ordnance Factories (POF)	Pakistan
Para-Ordnance Manufacturing Inc	Canada
Patria	Finland
Productos Mendoza	Mexico
Pindad	Indonesia
Rafael Advanced Defense Systems (Rafael)	Israel
Rangemaster Precision Arms	UK
Remington Arms (Remington)	USA
Rheinmetall AG (Rheinmetall)	Germany
RND Manufacturing	USA
Rock River Arms	USA
Romtehnica	Romania
Rosoboronexport	Russia
Royal Ordnance	UK
Royal Aquarius Defense Industries	USA
RPC Fort (Fort)	Ukraine
S&T Daewoo	South Korea
Saab AB	Sweden
SAKO	Finland
Samsung Techwin	South Korea
Savage Arms	USA
Sellier & Bellot	Czech Republic
Serbu Firearms	USA
Sharps Rifle Manufacturing Company	USA
Smith & Wesson (S&W)	USA
Springfield Armory (former U.S. Army arsenal)	USA
Springfield Armory (modern company)	USA
Sphinx Systems Ltd.	Switzerland
Sterling Armaments Company	UK
Steyr Mannlicher (Steyr)	Austria
ST Engineering	Singapore
STI International	USA

Stoeger Industries	Italy
Strayer Voigt Inc	USA
Sturm, Ruger, & Co. (Ruger)	USA
Swiss Arms (US subsidiary known as SIG Sauer)	Switzerland
Thai Aviation Industry	Thailand
THOR Global Defense Group	USA
TsNIITochMash	Russia
Thompson	USA
Turkish Aerospace Industries (TAI)	Turkey
Taser International	USA
Forjas Taurus (Taurus)	Brazil
TEREM	Bulgaria
Textron Systems (Textron)	USA
Thompson Center Arms (Thompson Center)	USA
Thales Group (Thales)	France
ThyssenKrupp	Germany
U.S. Fire Arms Manufacturing Company (U.S. Fire Arms Mfg. Co.; USFA)	USA
U.S. Repeating Arms Company (USRAC)	Belgium
Uralvagonzavod (UVZ)	Russia
Winchester Repeating Arms Company	Belgium
Walther	Germany
Webley & Scott	UK
W. W. Greener	UK
Valmet	Finland
Yuzhnoye Design Bureau	Ukraine
Zastava Arms	Serbia

In 2011 these corporations received over half a trillion (more than 500 billion) dollars in U.S. government contracts to make weapons, want to guess how much went into education? *77 billion*. To date the cost of running both the wars in Iraq and Afghanistan are nearing 4 trillion, We The American People were told that the war in Iraq would never top 1 trillion.

Section 8
The Wealth Transfer Scheme

Despite the propagation of lies being spread by most of the mainstream media outlets as well as the further lies by omission, the global financial and economic conditions are dire and getting worse every day. There has never been any type of economic recovery status post the bursting of the housing bubble and subsequent fallout here in the United States what so ever, and here is why. Outright in our faces asset, economic, and financial manipulation by the Federal Reserve. The politicocorporatists realized that they had stumbled upon an opportunity which would generate more wealth for them than they ever could have imagined, by stealthily stealing the wealth from the largest portion of society-the middle class. Furthermore it would be as easy as taking candy from a baby.

The Federal Reserve and other world central banks have already totally and completely brainwashed the vast majority of the population into believing that pieces of paper with numbers printed on them represent real wealth. So again the great majority of people on a global scale are ready and willing to labor, sweat, and sacrifice for some of that paper. Subsequently the world central banks are well aware of that concept.

This plain fact remains: paper is paper and every bill printed by world central banks are simply this, unbacked liabilities being distributed by bankrupt governments. These liabilities have no real value at all, and this is the beauty of it for the world's central bankers. These central banks who are now the largest purchasers of gold in the world, are acquiring gold in mass with the monies earned from interest on their printed out of thin air worthless paper. It truly is the greatest theft in world history. It gets better.

As the market crash of 2008 progressed, the Wall Street insiders in direct collusion with the central banks came up a monumental plan, they figured out a way to turn this collapse into the greatest wealth transfer scheme the world had ever seen! With the bursting of the housing bubble and subsequent stock market crash of 2008 we found out that major banks, mortgage companies, and various other institutions has made bad bets in the asset markets and lost staggering amounts of cash. In fact they lost this wealth using their clients' monies in many instances and were leveraging that debt as much as 50 to 1. Gambling pure and simple. This same situation has continued on a global level and not just here in the United States.

So what happened? Well these institutions were not allowed to take these losses so they got bailed out using public funds. This same situation is continuing even now as we are witnessing these same events in Europe. These institutions were and are continuing to be "made whole." In fact they are being made whole to the tune of hundreds of trillions of dollars and this debt is now owed by YOU. Yes, and this is why we are seeing our standard of living plummet while the cost of it keeps rising. How do you feel about that? The people of Europe and soon the world are also being forced to endure austerity so this debt can be paid back. This same situation although much worse is going to occur right here in America and why? Because here in the U.S. we have the biggest debt issue of them all, so the price which must be paid will be much higher.

Believe it or not, although you are being forced with no recourse to cover the bad bets made by the investment banks and other institutions you have actually been getting robbed since the day of your birth, please allow me to explain. As we know all fiat monetary systems which is the model for all modern economies globally, is based upon the perpetual acquisition of debt. In fact currency is actually and simply borrowed into existence and therefore is debt itself.

Public debt which is also known as sovereign debt also called the national debt is the overall indebtedness of a particular nation. As a citizen of that said nation you "own" a part of that debt. For example, at the time of this writing the public debt here in the United States is $15,943,000,000,000. A child born on this day at this hour as a U.S. citizen from the moment of his/her birth is a born debtor owning and owing $50,770 of the public debt. As soon as that child begins his/her first job and begins to pay taxes that number will triple. If you are an American citizen and a taxpayer the amount of debt you now owe towards the national deficit at the time of this writing is nearly $150,000. Also at this time the total national debt of nearly sixteen trillion dollars exceeds the total GDP or gross national product, which is the total amount of goods and services created in one year. What this means is as a nation the U.S. must now borrow even more cash at a faster rate just to maintain the current state of affairs in this country. Also at the time of this writing the unemployment rate here in the U.S. is 8.3%, the GDP is 1.5%, and a college graduates average salary has dropped 5% since the crash of 2008. In fact on average the net worth lost by the American public is 38%.

America is the biggest debtor nation in the history of the world, a far cry from where we were status post WWII when America was by far the richest nation the world had ever known. America under inept leadership has had her wealth literally stolen, and it is going to get much worse. Since the inception of central banking in 1913 the U.S. Dollar has lost 98% or its purchasing power. This accelerated when were were stripped of our gold standard in 1971. This is also why the standard of living for people not just here in America but globally have seen their standard of living fall, and why it usually requires 2 incomes to support a family.

What the vast majority fail to realize is prices rise because the value of currency falls, it is not that the asset or item became more valuable, it is that the currency became worth less. Now what central banks do is set a target interest rate, for example in the U.S. at this time the Federal Reserve has a target rate for inflation of near 2.5%. Just to give you an idea of how this is yet another example of how the Fed. is stealing our cash currently, the Fed. estimated GDP at 1.5% meanwhile they have a target rate of 2.5% for inflation! Does this make any sense to you at all?! It is theft by stealth, the general public has simply no idea that they are being robbed. Furthermore, at this time any person who has a savings account is also being fleeced by the Fed. And here is why. Interest being paid on savings accounts here in the U.S. is being paid at less than the projected rate of inflation! Again, theft via stealth.

Lets move on. The global financial situation is so grave at this time that people, foreign governments, corporations, etc. are still buying U.S. government debt even though these bonds themselves are again paying less than the projected rate of inflation. Think about that for a moment, the holders of U.S debt realize (unless they are dopey) that by holding a U.S. T-bill they are guaranteed to lose wealth. Incredible isn't it? After the bursting of the housing bubble and subsequent crash of 2008 the price of gold rose from about $700 an ounce to over $1,600 at this present time. The world's central banks who are the very entities who print (fiat) out of thin air and distribute that paper have been the largest buyers of gold since the crash of 2008. Does that surprise you? They themselves do not believe in the very thing which they produce for the aggregate people to hold! If you follow my daily video blog on YouTube you would have heard me repeat what I am about to say right now; BECOME YOUR OWN CENTRAL BANK and get out of fiat on a global level. Actually I do advocate holding the Chinese Renminbi and why is that? I firmly believe that the Chinese will be the next to hold the world's reserve currency because the U.S. Dollar has been destroyed. I also believe that the Chinese will also be backing the Renminbi with gold in the future.

Just for a moment think of what that will mean for the U.S. Dollar and the American way of life. Overnight the dollars value will plummet and the cost of living here in the United States will double, or worse. People foolishly believe that the U.S. Dollar will always be the reserve currency, this type of thinking is typical and unrealistic. As of this writing the United Stated must borrow nearly half of every dollar it spends, and a full 25% of the total taxes collected in the U.S. go to paying just the interest in the debt, a debt which typically doubles every 5 to 7 years. So what will happen to the American way of life in say 7 years when the national deficit doubles and 50% of taxes have to go to paying just the interest on the debt? It simply cannot be and it is unsustainable.

Section 9

Every Debt Based Economy Will Fail Over Time

What must be understood before moving forward is this simple fact; any and every economic model which is based upon the accumulation of debt in perpetuity is guaranteed to fail. As we now know, this scheme is the model which has been "adopted" by virtually every modern economy in the world today. Debt based economic models built around fiat (unbacked), financial systems have been tried since ancient times and never once has one been successful and subsequently they always fail, even the fall of Rome was brought about for this reason. In modern times we have witnessed the failure of nine fiat based economic systems and they are listed as follows: Germany Weimer Republic 1922-1923, Hungary 1945-1946, Chile 1971-1981, Argentina 1975-1992, Peru 1988-1991, Angola 1991 -1999, Yugoslavia 1992-1995, Belarus 1994-2002, and Zimbabwe 2000-2009.

In each of these instances massive and hyperinflation caused each of these systems to fail and be replaced, ironically by other fiat systems. It seems that we never learn doesn't it? Or is there something else going on. Today we are witnessing the simultaneous death of the Euro and the U.S. Dollar, the currency of two of the world's major economic engines. The ramifications of this event are going to shake the world. The main issue with this situation today is never before in the history of the world has a failing fiat currency been the world reserve-the U.S. Dollar. Many nations of the world are preparing themselves for the replacement of the U.S. Dollar as the world reserve. Most notably of these are Brazil, China, India, Russia, South Africa and Japan. Each of these countries has already or is in the process of eliminating the U.S. Dollar in their trade. Furthermore, even other countries are considering abandoning the U.S. Dollar as well. Included in these countries are United Arab Emirates, Iran, and even Saudi Arabia.

In fact China and Saudi Arabia are jointly building the largest oil refinery in the history of the world, and it is scheduled to come online in 2014. It seems that the least aware of this fact are the citizens themselves who are simply not being told of the monumental changes which are happening all around them. Arguably the least aware of any of this are the American people as a whole. Sadly the vast majority of people exist in a purposely dumbed down, fantasy land, dream like state, a mindset which is easily manipulated.

What is being set up is a very grave situation involving the U.S. Dollar, which will soon be among the ranks of failed monetary systems. As the demand for the U.S. Dollar is falling on a global level the U.S. Federal Reserve keeps printing more dollars. This is creating a serious supply and demand issue for these dollars. This situation causes inflation and in this particular case will lead to hyperinflation.

As the U.S. Dollar continues to lose its status as the world reserve this problem is going to keep getting worse. This is going to lead to higher prices for goods and services across the board, but especially food and energy. Countries around the world are well aware of this concept and as stated are preparing accordingly. In fact the accumulation of gold by not just governments of the world, but also the central banks who themselves print the world's fiat currencies is at all time record highs. The issue is this, a serious conflict of interest. The world's central banks who at the same time are issuing "fake" wealth in the form of fiat capital to the peoples of the world are also the largest accumulators of gold on the planet. The more fiats they simultaneously print the higher the price of gold will go. This situation is also going to affect commodities across the board, but gold as well as silver are going to be the prime beneficiaries of this scheme.

Why is that? One might ask. Simple, gold and silver have been monetary instruments for thousands of years and just because the world's central banks that have a vested interest in stating that gold and silver are no longer money does not make it so. I also fully expect crude oil as well as corn to rise to highs which will be shocking to most. China is now positioning to fully capitalize on the unraveling economies of the western world. It is my firm belief that China is going to be backing their currency with gold and the ramifications of this is going to be catastrophic for the already dying U.S. Dollar as the world's reserve. China who has been the prime purchaser of U.S. debt, is now betting against the U.S. Dollar by taking up short positions. What this means is China is fully prepared to capitalize on the weakening and eventual failure of the U.S. Dollar and will make staggering profits from it, more than enough to cover their losses which will occur with their investments in U.S. Treasury bonds.

China also is well aware that the world's central banks are going to continue to print epic sums of fiat to push off and profit from (because their holdings in gold will explode to the upside), the collapse of their fiat currency.

The issue on a global level is that of debt. Once an economic model based on the perpetual accumulation of debt can no longer accrue any more debt, a crisis occurs. Meanwhile the policymakers in collusion with the central banks and corporate insiders continue to add debt through stimulus and bailouts, and neither of these will help solve the problem. A debt problem cannot be solved by adding more debt. Furthermore, bailing out/making whole failing institutions like banks and corporations for making "bad bets" is a surefire way of making the initial problem monumentally worse for the citizens who are now responsible for all of this new added debt.

The plain truth is this, the initial debt could not be repaid which means any and all debts which were subsequently added will certainly not be able to be paid back either, it is a very simple concept to understand.

It seems that the world leaders would be able to figure this one out on their own and make no mistake about it, they are well aware that this is in fact the case. No amount of bailout, stimulus, or even debt restructuring can fix this problem and that is a fact. What this means is a pan-global economic collapse is a mathematical certainty. What most people fail to realize is the monies which were used and lost by the world's banks was not their own, but that of their customers, in other words-your capital. Not only have these institutions used your cash to gamble with in a variety of obviously losing endeavors, they have leveraged it as much as 50X. What this means is each of these institutions is insolvent despite what monies may show up on their balance sheets.

Moreover, being that they have literally gambled away your wealth you are insolvent as well. If you are a follower of my daily blog on YouTube you have probably heard me say repeatedly to get your cash out of these bankrupt institutions and become your own central bank.

What I strongly suggest and advocate is doing exactly what the central banks are doing, and that is give yourself a DE-facto gold standard. Holding precious metals in this type of global environment is the number one way to protect yourself from failing currencies. Furthermore, not only is holding gold and silver the best possible way to preserve your wealth in an environment where the currency is being debased, it is also the greatest way to grow your wealth multiple fold as this crisis deepens. At the present time globally we are experiencing the early phases of this collapse.

We are witnessing deleveraging across the board with equities, as well as commodities. But again, this is just the initial phase. What must be understood is the only thing which the world central banks can and will do to accomplish their goals is print fiat.

In fact, even though here in the United States alone the Federal Reserve has increased the monetary base over 300% since the crash of 2008 this is just the beginning. Despite the fact that the U.S. Dollar is losing its reserve status and as such the demand for these dollars is falling, the Federal Reserve will continue to print more. This scenario is always the same at the end of every prior failed currency; capital is printed out of thin air to the point where it becomes worthless. Some would ask why the Federal Reserve doesn't just stop printing? An excellent question actually and here is the answer. Being that each dollar is just a unit of debt, and the entire U.S. economy (and that of every fiat based system) is based upon the continual and relentless accumulation of debt, if the Federal Reserve stops printing that would mean the debt accumulation would stop and the entire system would collapse overnight. This is also the main reason why the Federal Reserve will not allow the current deflationary cycle to continue.

The Federal Reserve as well as the other world's central banks will print epic sums of cash to prevent any real deflation. In the end the U.S. Dollar as well as every other fiat based economic model will join the ranks of failed currencies. It is my firm belief that a return to sound money, that is a monetary system backed by a hard asset like gold is an eventuality. The collapse of the current corrupted system will be the reset button. Can you now understand why countries cannot balance their budgets? A debt based economic model must simply and continually accumulate more and more debt; the policymakers no doubt fully comprehend this concept but are unable to share this "secret" with the public.

Nevertheless, imagine for a moment what would happen if President Obama got on international media and said: *"we cannot balance the budget because our current economic model demands an ever increasing amount of debt, and at the moment we balance the budget the entire system will collapse overnight."*

Section 10
The X-Wave Phenomenon

I consider myself to be a financial tactician, I started out working in this financial game in the early 1990's as a technical analyst. I got to witness and work on Wall Street during the dot-com bubble and I have had opportunities to work with and be taught by brilliant financial minds. I owe each of them a great deal of gratitude.

As a financial tactician I constantly study the world markets, looking for fundamental changes in policy, gauging what the next moves will most likely be by governments, central banks, and major corporations. By understanding who the major players are in this financial gamy and realizing their goals, it makes it simpler to predict what their next moves will most likely be with a high degree of probability.

My job as a financial tactician is to analyze a great deal of information and put it all together like a puzzle, searching for clues in a way to back up what my hypothesis already is. An integral part of this reasoning is peering at charts, looking for patterns, or deviations from expected patterns and ascertaining what it all means. This is in no way an easy thing to do but by following my own algorithm throughout the years I have had a success rate of about 90%. What this means is yes, I have a near 10% margin of error, but statistically the odds are well in my favor. Again, if I had not stood upon the shoulders of giants I would have never been able to attain anywhere near the success I have achieved.

After the bursting of the housing bubble and subsequent crash of the global markets the financial insiders (Wall Street), in direct collusion with central bankers and our policymakers realized that their was an unbelievable opportunity for more wealth to be made in one simple transaction than in all of human history. Subsequently what was schemed into existence is doing exactly that. Prior to the crash of 2008 the U.S. and the world seemed to be firing on all cylinders, the unemployment rate was 4.6%, and GDP (gross domestic product) was 4.92 then...party over.

In one fell swoop the bottom dropped out of the hyperinflated housing prices and the grossly inflated equity markets took a nose dive. Banks, other institutions, and investors, took massive losses across the board. The DOW went from a euphoric high of 14,270 to a low of 6,460 all in the span of two and a half years. Now the DOW may have dropped further if it were not for direct intervention by the Federal Reserve, but this decision was in no way intended to help the American people. In an unprecedented move the Federal Reserve and the U.S. Treasury Department decided to institute massive bailouts for the banks and corporations who took heavy losses. This was known as the TARP program, something we went over earlier in this book. This action used public funds to bail out private banks and other corporations. At that particular point in time the last gasp of breath of a free market economy was taken. Understand in a free and capitalistic society those who made bad business decisions are supposed to fail and subsequently new and better business models are expected to emerge, but this was never allowed to happen. What did come of this was a totally new type of government was installed, a corporate state controlled by the government, also known as Fascism. The last time a fascist government was a major world power the leaders wore swastikas on their arms, massive death and human suffering on an unimaginable scale also took place. Well,it it happening all over again, the U.S. military is now used as a weapon of mass terror to be pointed at anyone who opposes the will of those in power, and I am not just talking about another nation or rogue state, I am referring to the American people.

In May of 2012 the U.S. Defense Department began to seek authority to authorize the deployment of the military to police American streets. However, the Posse Comitatus Act, Section 1385, states explicitly that only under specific circumstances expressly authorized by the Constitution or an act of Congress can the military presence on American streets be allowed.

However if the U.S. Defense Department has their way a new defense authorization act for fiscal year 2013 will give them the power to order the armed forces to be used against the American public. President Obama has already expressed his support for this provision because already on December 31, 2011 President Obama signed into law the National Defense Authorization Act (NDAA) for Fiscal Year 2012. In this act there were put in place provisions for not only using the U.S. military against the American people, but also sections allowing for the unlimited detention of American people on American soil without trial or jury!

Thankfully the sections of this act which allowed for these actions was found to be a perversion of the Constitution and an overreach of Presidential power, subsequently these sections were stricken down at that time. But, it seems that neither the Department of Defense nor the President has given up in further pursuit of these additions to the NDAA of 2013. The simple fact that 1. The President would initially sign such an act for 2012, and that 2. The DOD is still pursuing these additions is truly frightening. Why would they even consider using the military to police the streets of America? We will cover that later on in this book.

Wall Street finally now has a type of government which would ensure that their financial goals would be met, with a puppet President and a Congress which would bow to their will. **While the American people were being distracted by the falling values of their homes and 401K plans, installing a new type of government would be as simple as taking a stroll on a quiet suburban street on a beautiful spring day..and they did it just like that.**

So how has this all played out? Lets consider the following: instead of the Federal Reserve and the Treasury department simply allowing natural free market forces to dictate the fair market value of equities, commodities, and real estate, Fed. Chairman Ben Bernanke (who is also a direct puppet of Wall Street) initiated what is known as quantitative easing. Quantitative easing is simply this: monetary policy utilized to increase the currency supply by 1. Buying government securities (bonds), 2. Buying other securities from the market (like stocks and other assets) and 3. Flooding financial institutions with liquidity (cash) to encourage lending.

The leading risk of quantitative easing is more cash is made available but the demand for the currency does not increase and this will eventually lead to higher prices across the board (inflation). In the case of the United States we have already had two outright episodes of failed QE. The first round was initiated when the DOW hit 6,500. When that failed to stimulate the economy we got QE2, and when that also failed to stimulate the economy we got operation twist, (*which is just an idiotic name for bond swaps*) the Federal Reserve selling short term bonds and buying long term bonds with the currency. Now, we found out that the Fed. is going to extend operation twist until the end of 2012 and why? Because the first operation twist also failed to stimulate the economy. What was the cost to you and me for all this (the American people)? 1.7 trillion for QE1, another 1.7 trillion for QE2, another half a trillion for the first operation twist, and another quarter of a trillion for operation twist (squared). Truly staggering amounts of capital to say the least. But let's for a moment look at this just a bit closer. Who has really benefited from all this cash being printed out of thin air? Well we realize that it is not the American people as the numbers regarding unemployment and inflation are so bad that the government must lie about them. For example, at this time the government is stating that the unemployment rate is 8.3%, but the actual numbers are closer to 16%.

Government numbers regarding inflation are just 1.7%. But consider this, year over year 2011-2012 the cost of food and prescription drugs have increased faster than the government's inflation measure, rising 3.56 %, 4.21 % respectfully! Natural gas and electricity have also increased at 2.74%.

The real beneficiaries of quantitative easing have been global market speculators, the investment banks, and the corporations. Allow me to explain, the cost for these institutions to borrow capital and subsequently speculate with it in the markets is next to nil. They can simply borrow all this extra liquidity, leverage it, and then speculate with it almost for free. This is why the equity markets have "rebounded" from their lows after the crash of 2008. Now that the markets are "front run" by the Fed., (*that is the practice of trading an equity based on information unavailable to the public, also known as insider trading*) huge amounts of cash are able to be made by these institutions.

The curious thing is this, everyone who has been involved in the markets as long as I have realizes this practice of front running takes place every day and yet nothing is being done about it. It is also no secret that institutions like JP Morgan in collusion with the CME group manipulate the prices of precious metals and again, nothing is done about that either.

The best way anyone can protect themselves from all this manipulation and currency printing on a global level is to hold gold and silver and become your own central bank. Because we realize the charade we ourselves can capitalize on the situation. In truth there are many ways to do this some requiring more effort than others, but for me I like to take the most straightforward and safe way. Lets consider this chart below.

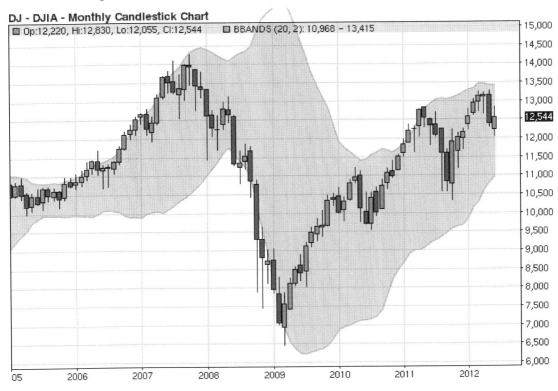

This chart is the DOW from 2005 until July 2012.

Next is that same chart in which I have circled the market top prior to the 2008 crash and the bottom. Following the crash you can appreciate the effects of QE1, QE2, and operation twist.

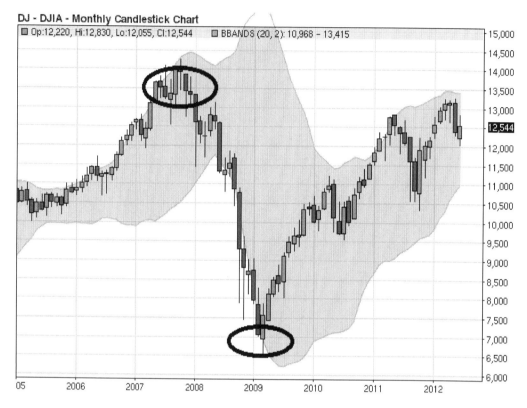

If you follow the trend line from the bottom you will notice a drop off in the middle of 2010, this is where QE1 ended, notice the market reaction/pullback. Now follow the next leg up, that was QE2, and the pullback is where that ended as well. The last leg up is where operation twist was instituted and the pullback is where twist (one) is ending right now. Operation twist 2 is beginning now.

From looking at this chart it is clear that had it not been for direct market manipulation by the Federal Reserve the overall markets would not be anywhere near to the point they are today.

Below is a chart of the S&P 500, which is a much broader market index in that it contains 500 companies instead of the DOW which only consists of 30.

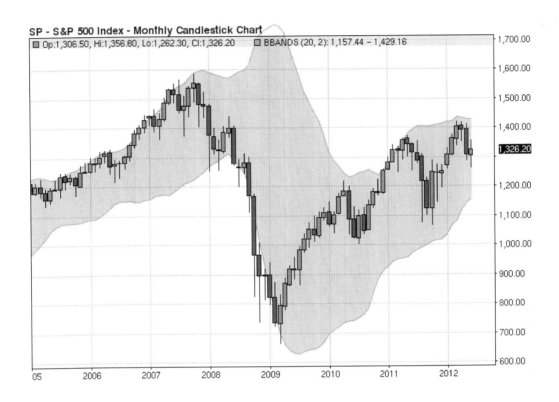

If you look at both of the previous charts, that of the DOW and S&P 500, you will notice an almost exact pattern.

Now below is yet another chart, this one is of gold during the same time periods, that is 2005 through until July 2012.

If you look at this chart of gold above you will see that this trend line is nearly linear despite all the market turmoil over this period of time. This is because gold is the most stable asset the world has ever known, and because of that fact huge amounts of information can be gleaned by basing the performance of other assets and even entire indexes like the DOW and S&P 500 against gold.

In this next chart I have again taken gold, same time line, however I have placed trend lines in 2 specific places.

This first trend line was just prior and through the crash of 2008, notice the incredible bull run gold made to date. It went from $700oz to just shy of $1,600 in just 3.5 years. It is my firm belief that we are nearing another massive leg up in gold as well as another 2008 (or worse) stock market crash. Here is my reasoning on this. As we know since the market bottom early 2009 up until now, the Federal Reserve has been directly involved in propping up the equity markets with quantitative easing. What this has done is create a fake environment across the board in equity markets globally.

As another example of this lets look at another chart. This next one is again the S&P 500 which I have divided into two half's one prior to the crash of 2008 and the aftermath. I have also placed two horizontal lines representing current economic conditions on either side of the crash.

On the left side of this chart at the horizontal line the unemployment rate was an excellent 4.6%, GDP was again a strong 4.92. The average yearly salary for a new college graduate was $45K.

Now, on the right side of this chart of the S&P 500 horizontal line, *note the same level in the index of 1,326 where we are today*, the unemployment rate is an awful 8.3%, GDP a miserable 1.5, and the average salary of a new college graduate has fallen to 40K from 45K.

What must also be known is on average the net worth of the aggregate American public has dropped by a staggering 38% status post crash of 2008.

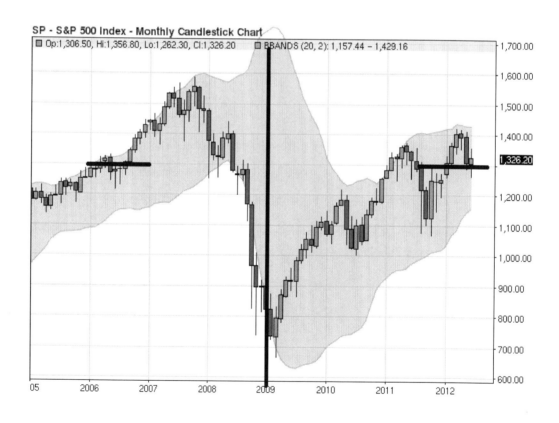

Now, if you were to base the value of either the DOW or the S&P 500 against these current economic conditions here in the U.S. you can easily surmise that these indexes are grossly overvalued and hyperinflated. If you follow the financial channels you will hear many commentators discuss market valuation. In order to gauge what they are referring to in this context, it is market value taking into account future growth potential. That is not actually basing it against the CURRENT economic conditions. Now, we heard a lot of this talk just prior to the crash of 2008 and many of these same commentators were predicting DOW 20,000. So in my opinion in order to correctly understand what the true market valuation is, it must be weighted against current economic conditions and not any projected future valuation. If one were to take into account the current quickly deteriorating global economic conditions and contrast the massive amount of propping up/manipulation of the markets by the Federal Reserve it is simple to see that this market is due for a major crash. Understand, the sole job of the markets is to determine the fair market value of a particular asset, that's it. Now, at one point it will be the market which will determine these values because market forces are enormous and no amount of manipulation by the central banks globally will be able to overpower those forces over time.

Now that we realize that the market is highly overvalued, and that future economic conditions will continue to deteriorate it is easy to understand true market valuation. We also realize that the global debt issue cannot be resolved by any of the means being tried at this time. Furthermore, if there was a way it could have been fixed they would have done it by now. All of the global world leaders are well aware that the situation is dire and a global economic/financial collapse is now unavoidable. In fact it is now being fostered to happen with purpose. To bring about the greatest transfer of wealth the world has ever seen.

When I first introduced my X-Wave theory I must say I was quite surprised with regard to the amount of positive feedback I received. Initially I thought most people would disagree with it however it seems that today more and more people are becoming more aware that something on a global scale is dreadfully wrong.

My hypothesis for this phenomenon began sometime in 2011 when I began to notice peculiar distortions in long term charts, and then gauging that information against current market trends. What its end result was is this, a particular convergence/divergence with regard to the value of the DOW and gold, see the chart below.

The first time this particular convergence/divergence occurred during the crash of 2008 is noted by the first circled area, *the black line is gold during the same time period.* It appears that this same phenomenon is occurring again right now, see the second circled area.

What we know from the fundamental side is the market is again highly overvalued and due for a correction. We also realize that globally, which includes the United States, economic conditions are continuing to deteriorate. We also realize that the extension of operation twist, which I like to call operation twist squared, is not going to change the trajectory of the current slowing U.S. economy. It is my suspicion that the Federal Reserve is going to initiate another round of overt stimulus (official QE3) at the end of operation twist squared and at that point the world will come to the grim realization that no amount of stimulus is going to be able to push off the collapse any longer. Fear will then take over the markets and bond yields will rise pushing up interest rates. This will put massive pressure on equities which will sell off, and subsequently all of this cash is going to look for a place to go and that place is going to be commodities.

Therefore this X-Wave Phenomenon is telling me that gold as well as commodities across the board are going to spike and the value of the U.S. Dollar is going to plummet. The convergence stage of this "X-Wave" is occurring now and the divergence phase will occur in the not so distant future. A major market crash is on the horizon.

Section 11
The Scope Of This Is Immense

On a global scale status post the crash of 2008, the biggest financial institutions in the world have been operating with negative balance sheets. What this means is they are bankrupt and therefore the people are bankrupt as well. However, most don't even realize it. *Theft by stealth.* What has and is happening is truly gargantuan in its scope, and in truth the party ended in 2008. Ever since 2008 the global economies have been literally on life support and this can be seen simply by gauging that without the intervention by the Federal Reserve as well as the other world central banks, the world as we know it would literally cease to exist.

Prior to the crash of 2008 financial institutions were issuing credit and mortgages to anyone with a heartbeat, and they did not care one iota if these borrowers were able to bay back these loans. The scheme worked like this, a lender would package a loan then sell this loan to another financial institution, very simple. In this manner the initial lender would be made whole immediately and pull out a profit while the now secondary holder of that said loan/mortgage would be stuck holding that bad loan. These are known as an MBS or more commonly "mortgage backed securities." Subsequently even these "securities" (which were already known to be bad) were sold to other investors. These loans were sold off to other parties as derivatives and put into tranches (a portion of several related securities with various risks, rewards and/or maturities). Now, the holders of these loans and MBS would now through derivatives trades leverage this debt multiple times. This would result in catastrophic losses (on the long end) of these transactions via these initial prepackaged "sub-prime" mortgages and loans. However, the grand scheme in this was to actually take advantage of the short end (that is betting against) these bad loans and that is exactly what happened.

Understand, in any financial transaction cash is never really lost. Wealth does not simply disappear into "money" heaven and there are always two sides of a transaction. If one party is "betting" an asset is going to rise (go long) there is always some other party on the short end, that is betting against it. So if in the case of a MBS if one party is holding the long end, someone else is holding the short end of the trade. Somebody loses and somebody wins, period. The cash simply passes from one party to another. The crash of 2008 made some people and institutions wealthy beyond imagination and in the end what happened? Well the Federal Reserve and the U.S. Treasury Department simply made these banks and mortgage companies whole using public monies, your capital, exactly what they wanted. So now do you understand how Wall Street rules the world?

It is common knowledge that the world's central banks and even governments like China are increasing their holdings of physical gold faster than they ever have before. Actually up until 2008 the world's central banks were net sellers of gold, so what happened? Simple, they are betting against the dollar and more importantly against U.S. debt. Allow me to explain. One of the main reasons why I advocate holding gold and silver is it is the number one best hedge for betting against U.S. debt, global debt, and the inevitable total failure of the world's fiat monetary system(s).

The world's debt issues are truly epic, and if you were to factor in the debt derivatives markets we are talking about a global debt burden of over 1.5 quadrillion U.S Dollars and this continues to grow minute by minute and hour by hour. I am including in this number the total sum of sovereign debt (debt held by the public) as well. There is simply no way this sum can ever be paid back and as we are seeing already, the nations of Europe are on the cusp of defaulting on their sovereign debt. The U.S. will be the last country to fall- but it will fall as well. Keep in mind that a technical default has already occurred here in the U.S. because if it were not for the Fed. buying bonds an actual default would have already happened.

Holding precious metals is like having a short position against this global debt, and is the best way to capitalize on the situation bar none. Here in the United States the national debt is near 16 trillion dollars and historically the debt doubles every 5 to 7 years. At this time 25% of the taxes collected by the American people goes to pay just the interest on this debt.

When the debt doubles again, and it will, it will require 50% of the tax revenue to pay the debt and this is not sustainable, an outright debt default by the United States is a mathematical certainty. With this advanced knowledge the smart investors will be "shorting the debt" by holding precious metals. Understand, there is no escaping this. You can choose to either be on the long end of this transaction, that is stay in fiat, or take the short end and become your own central bank. As this unfolds the multiples which are going to be made with regard to real wealth by those betting against the debt by holding precious metals is going to be staggering. It is for this reason that central banks and world governments are now acquiring gold.

Global debt which includes derivatives eclipses the total amount of the existing fiat currency of every country in the world multiple fold. Even if you were to tax every person/business on the Earth at 100% it would take over ten thousand years for the current debt to be paid back. With this knowledge it is even clearer to see that a pan-global debt collapse is 100% guaranteed and we are seeing it happen right before our eyes. This situation of extreme debt is unfixable by any means and any efforts by world leaders to fix it is futile. Believe me if they could have fixed it this problem they would have done it by now. Countries like China, Russia, Japan, and others, who are major holders of U.S. debt via treasury bonds are hedging their bets by taking up massive short positions against the U.S. Dollar. China in particular is way out front with regard to this hedge and is well positioned to capitalize on a U.S. debt default and subsequent dollar collapse.

So we understand that status post the crash of 2008 the American people's wealth has dropped 38%, so understanding that capital does not simply vanish where do you think this staggering amount of wealth went? Well we realize that the richest 1% of the world continues to get richer while the rest continue to lose their net worth, so does that give you an idea of where all this abundance went? I really hope that you realize that this wealth transfer scheme is happening right under your nose and no one is talking about it. It is perception which must be kept in check by the global public, belief that this issue of wealth destruction is happening for everyone is paramount and nothing could be further from the truth. The middle class world wide is being taken to the cleaners while the rich take advantage of this "God given" gift, that was the crash of 2008 and its subsequent fallout. Furthermore, this issue is going to accelerate until the middle class on a world wide level no longer exists. I firmly believe that in the future there is going to be just two classes of people, an upper class and a lower class.

A ruling class and the surfs. Now my single premise is this, to get you on the winning side of this simple equation. Even more, to allow you to survive this transition. Understand and this is no joke, this is a life and death matter for a great proportion of the world's population, allow me to put a perspective on this. Being that we have borrowed from the future therefore creating epic amounts of debt to live a better life now, a future paradigm shift has been created, one which has the potential to have a terrible ending. For a moment ponder this: lets say you wanted to raise livestock, and to do this you took out a line of credit to initially obtain a few animals and create an environment which would be conducive to them procreating. After a period of time your livestock would multiply and perhaps you would have to expand the property for which they lived. Now lets say for example that your line of credit was cut, and subsequently you were unable to acquire the resources needed so sustain these animals of their current environment. What do you think would begin to happen to these animals? Simple, due to the lack of available resources they would begin to die off. Well on a global scale the same thing is going to happen to human beings. There is a direct correlation between the global debt and the current world wide population boom. Allow me to put a visual on this for you. This next chart is that of just the ballooning United States debt.

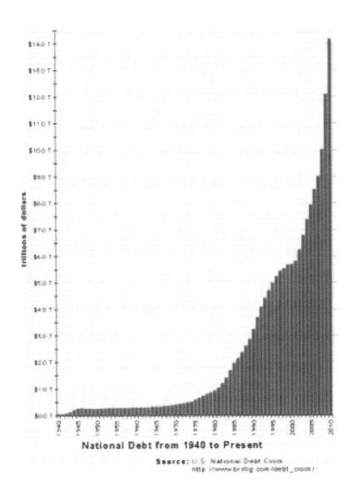

National Debt from 1940 to Present

Source: U.S. National Debt Clock
http://www.brillig.com/debt_clock/

Please observe how the debt curve began to increase after the abandonment of the gold standard and the establishment of the petrodollar, I placed a line at that particular time in the following chart.

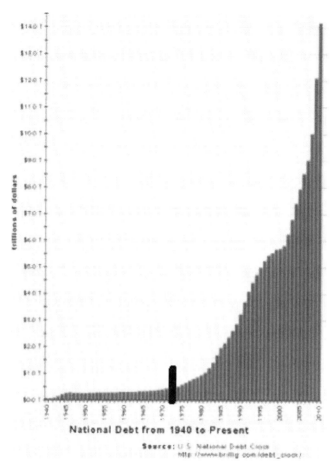

National Debt from 1940 to Present

Source: U.S. National Debt Clock
http://www.brillig.com/debt_clock/

Now, I would like you to look at this next chart. This is a chart representing the boom in the global population since that time, and I also placed a line representing where the gold standard was abandoned and the petrodollar was begun as well.

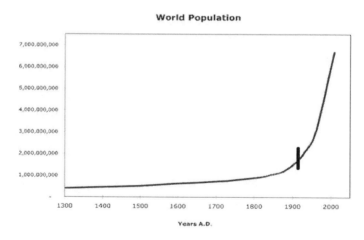

Do you see a similarity in the increasing curve/slope of these two previous charts? They are nearly identical.

152

So we understand that globally this debt is not sustainable and we also understand that the debt represents the largest economic/financial bubble the world has ever seen. The one fact which must be kept in mind is this: every economic/financial bubble in history has burst and this one will not be an exception.

Economic/financial bubbles all rise beyond a level which can be sustained by any means and they must burst. It is a simple mathematical certainty.

Below are examples of previous economic/financial bubbles which you may recall have burst in the recent past. Instead of writing about them, I thought I would simply put charts so you can get a visual-because you know what they say, a picture is worth a thousand words!

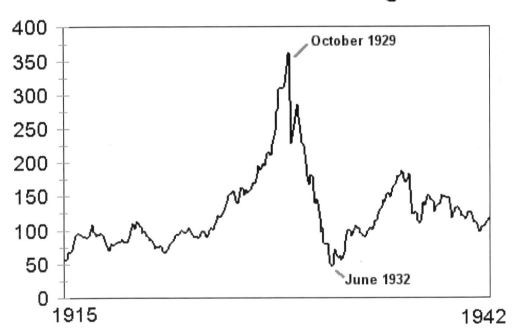

Dow-Jones Industrial Average

The Dot-Com Bubble.

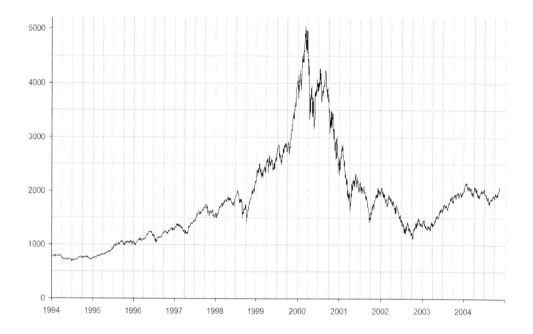

Again this next chart (following page) is the U.S. National Debt, do you notice any similarities between the slopes leading up to the bursting of the bubbles in these two previous charts?

U.S. National Debt Bubble Chart.

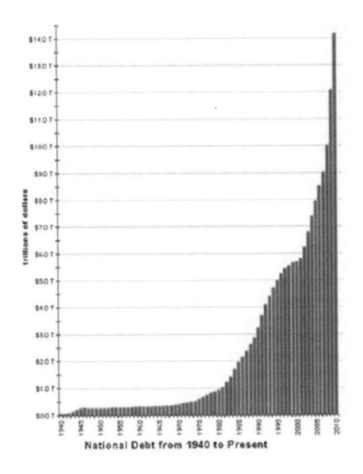

National Debt from 1940 to Present

World Population Bubble Chart.

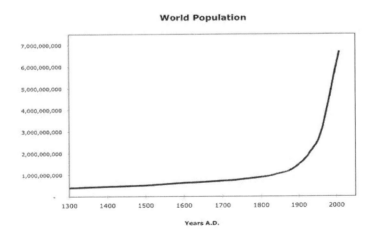

The similarities between all of these previous bubble charts rising slopes is uncanny. The simple fact is this, the global issue of debt is unresolvable without a complete collapse and resetting of the existing financial structure on a worldwide level. Realizing that this situation is now not just unavoidable but being fueled with purpose, (and that purpose is to continue to bring about the greatest transfer of wealth the world has ever seen), it is time for you as well to position yourself to benefit from this transaction as well-it is a matter of survival. Understand this does not make you a bad person, you are simply taking advantage of information which is available to anyone and making it work for you. Realize, if you do not take advantage of this position you will be setting yourself up to be taken advantage of those who are prepared to do so. Those who are fully prepared to take full advantage of the short end of the trade involving a global debt default are 1. The world's central banks, 2. Major countries like China, Russia, Japan, Brazil, India, and others. 3. Leading corporations, and 4. The richest 1% of the world's people, and 5. The world leaders.

In conclusion of this chapter, the entities mentioned in the previous paragraph are all fully prepared to "short this elephantine global debt bubble," and so should you. Bar none the most simple way to do this is to hold precious metals. In my opinion the most undervalued asset on the Earth at this time is physical silver. This one investment, silver, promises to pay off bigger than any other asset currently available to anyone on Earth at this time. Especially gauging that it is, along with gold, the single best way to short the global debt.

Section 12

A Two Tier Society Is Being Created

An incredible amount of public wealth has already been lost since the crash of 2008 and public funds are being used for bailout after bailout of financial institutions and even entire countries. Currency is being printed out of thin air in greater amounts than has ever been seen before by the world's central banks, therefore devaluing the currency. Currency devaluation takes away our purchasing power via inflation. These same financial institutions are paying negative returns on saving accounts thus once again stealing savers' wealth via stealth. Savings accounts are paying interest lower than the projected rate of inflation here in the United States. In fact the Federal Reserve has a target rate of inflation of 2.5% (and this is yet another reason why long term deflation is an impossibility), yet the average savings account in America is paying around 1%. So to put this into perspective there is an average loss of purchasing power of 1.5% per year compounded.

As of now societies are divided into three classes: the upper class, the middle class, and the lower class. I do not believe I have to elaborate further on the basis of this classification as it is more of less self explanatory. However, it is the middle class of which holds most of the wealth on average. While it is true that the richest 1% of society holds half the world's wealth, the other half is largely held by the middle class. The current state of financial affairs globally is literally consuming the wealth from the middle class at ever increasing rates. As the currency continues to be debased and purchasing power is being stolen, those who are positioned to benefit from this are certainly doing that. So who are the beneficiaries of this? Not just those who are currently rich, but those who are preparing now as well. In fact many people who hold their wealth in fiat, or more specifically believe that they have wealth in the form of fiat, are going to lose most of their wealth as we move forward.

People have an extremely hard time breaking old habits across the board. We are in a rapidly changing environment and the old ways of thinking regarding wealth creation and preservation simply will not work as we move further into the future. The equity markets are no longer based upon real valuation, but are readjusted almost on a daily basis with regard to what comes out of the mouths of central bankers and policymakers who both have a vested interest in seeing a specific outcome. Outcomes which usually go against the greater interests of the public. The entire system is now designed as a machine with one purpose, and that is to take from the unaware regardless of their current net worth. To steal directly from the pockets of those unable to think outside the box.

Out of the ashes of this global financial reset will come a new system built once again upon a sound money system. A system backed by a hard asset, most likely gold. This is nothing new, in fact going back through history the story is always the same.Although never before has a worldwide simultaneous collapse of the financial system occurred, and never has there been so much at stake.

I believe we are in the early stages of a transition period which will be very trying for a vast majority of the world's population, a situation where many will not get through in the literal sense. We are already witnessing a scramble for resources globally and as people continue to lose their purchasing power by the deliberate manipulation and debasement of the currency. Because of this and the inevitable prospect of massive and hyperinflation promising to sweep through the European continent and America a great deal of people are not going to be able to acquire basic necessities. This unavoidable situation is going to lead to collective social unrest, violent crime, and mass death.

The world's policymakers are well aware of these events and specifically this is why a police state is being created here in the United States as well as around the globe. Why else would the U.S. Department of Defense be seeking to police the streets of America with military forces? Why do we now have military drones patrolling our skies? Why did President Obama sign the National Defense Authorization (NDAA) Act of 2012 which would have allowed for American citizens to be arrested by the military on U.S. streets and also seek to imprison us indefinitely without trial or jury? Why are we no longer "One Nation Under God" but "One Nation Under Surveillance?" The answer is simple and clear, our policymakers understand that we are in a rapidly deteriorating global economic/financial death spiral of which there is no escaping. Only the strong will survive this, those of us who possess the foresight to see what is on the horizon have a chance to get to the other side of the global reset.

The world is in a great state of change, the middle class will be left to history as there will emerge a two tier system of haves and have-not's. In many ways this two tier system is a return to the past. In the grand scheme of things the middle class more or less emerged in the middle ages during the industrial revolution. Prior to the industrial revolution there existed two tier societies, a ruling class and those who serve that ruling class. There is no doubt that as this wealth transfer is complete this is exactly what will emerge once again. It can be said that by moving forward we are in fact moving backwards, back to a two tier society, back to a sound money system, back to a time where excess was not even available to most. One thing is for sure, the future is going to be interesting.

Section 13
Free Yourself From Debt Now!
Take Control of Your Life

If you are like most Americans you are in some kind of financial debt. Being in debt makes you an indentured servant. That is not only do you have to pay back the principal on the acquired loan but you also owe and subsequently are forced to service the compounding interest on that said loan over time. Having a debt burden is, let's face it, awful. So let's presume you have maxed out your credit card to the tune of five grand (a very easy thing to do by the way) and let's assume an annual interest rate of 10 percent. If you were to pay just the minimum each month it would take you forty years to pay it off, and with compounded interest over time that five thousand dollar line of credit will have cost you over forty thousand dollars! That is simply ridiculous my friend, and we are going to fix that problem right now.

Here are some basic statistics on the American people's unsecured credit card debt: as of this writing, the average credit card debt per household is: $16,000. There are over 600 million credit cards which are held by U.S. consumers. The average number of credit cards kept by cardholders is 3.5. The average Annual Percentage Rate (APR) on a new credit card offer is over 14.99 percent, *this kicks in after the initial low introductory rate and can go as high as 75% if a late payment is made.* The average APR on a credit card account with a balance on it is 13.00 percent. Total U.S. revolving debt, of which 98 percent is made up of credit card loans, is **almost a trillion dollars.**

Do you want to know a secret? If you hold unsecured debt defined as: *a loan **not** secured by an underlying asset or collateral, credit cards or anything else*, you have the legal right to liquidate over 60 percent of that said debt, and in some cases as much as 75 percent, just think about that that for a little while! This is no joke and millions of people have taken advantage of this and now it is your turn.

Yes you read that right and it does not matter what terms you agreed to, how much you make, whether you are working or not etc. etc. It took me a long time and a whole lot of blood sweat and tears to figure this little secret out, but before I understood how this credit game works I had gotten myself into well over $100,000.00 of debt, and now I am totally debt free. Not only am I totally debt free, but I now have a substantial net worth and have learned to create wealth for myself. And Now I am going to share with you how easy this all is to accomplish for yourself. It all comes down to this, a simple contract renegotiation. Something which is done each and every day.

Let us go over just three basic concepts to begin with. **First:** the banks and credit card issuers are all too eager to give out lines of credit as well as other unsecured loans and why is that? First of all they do not really care if you pay them back or not and that is the truth. Would they prefer if you did pay them back? Yes, because as an alternative of just breaking even on the loan/line of credit, they would instead make cash on the said loan. However, if an individual defaults on a loan the issuer does not lose capital and here is why: each time credit is issued to an individual the lender takes out insurance on that said loan which is paid for by the borrower in hidden fees associated with the terms of the unsecured loan. What this means is if the loan goes into default for whatever reason someone else is now responsible for that loan or credit. How much this insurance costs is based upon the borrowers credit score, and this is why an individual with a higher credit score is able to acquire a better interest rate, very simple. Actually the responsibility for a said loan is often shared between two or more parties depending on the size of the loan and it is commonly known as a Credit Default Swap. **Second:** The cash which was loaned out never really existed in the first place! If you have gotten through the earlier parts of this book you understand that currency is loaned into existence as debt and is printed out of thin air. However lets do a short review, here is how it works and it all starts with the Federal Reserve. The Federal Reserve which is not a part of the government and is in fact owned by other private banks sole purpose is to make a profit period.

161

And how does the Federal Reserve make a profit you might ask? A very good question! The Federal Reserve issues public debt in the form of a fiat monetary system. The Federal Reserve creates currency from nothing, that is it simply prints fiat or in the case of our digital world today simply adds currency to the public monetary base by adding zeros on a computer screen. This now newly created fiat is then owed back to the Federal Reserve/central bankers plus any interest it may accrue. Each and every fiat (which means "so let it be") dollar is then **owned** and **owed back** to the Federal Reserve. In reality each dollar which exists in the world today digital or otherwise is an IOU made payable directly to the central bankers/Federal Reserve plus interest. *So the Federal Reserve creates capital from nothing and issues nothing but debt, and that is how they make wealth for themselves.*

On a grander scale, how this cash which is created from nothing makes its way to the consumer/you is this. The Fed. creates this fiat which is then distributed to the banks. The Fed. then begins to charge the bank interest on this new currency backed by nothing and literally printed out of thin air (or digitally added to a computer screen) which is then loaned to you at a premium. So especially in the cases today where everything is digital, the cash which is being loaned out does not even exist, it is an illusion. As we know prior to 1971 the United States did not have a fiat monetary system, we had a gold standard. What this means is every single dollar/coin in existence was backed by gold and silver which was stored in government stockpiles. In fact what most people fail to realize is today because of fiat monetary systems, we have "debt based economies." **What a debt based economy does is create debtors, not wealth.** Therefore prior to 1971/going off a gold standard, we did not have a debt based economy, what we had was an economy based upon the creation of wealth for the citizens as well as our country as a whole.

Today your paycheck is backed by no hard asset, and as such the purchasing power of the dollar has plummeted. A dollar in 1971 will buy you about 18 cents of the same items today. Since 2008 the Federal Reserve has increased the monetary base over 300% and continues to do so, what this means is each new dollar printed by the Fed. continues to devalue each dollar, digital or otherwise, in existence. So not only is the Fed. issuing debt and creating debtors, each passing day that the Fed. prints currency you are getting poorer by having your purchasing power stolen from you. Since just 2008 the purchasing power of your dollar has lost 15 percent of its value, and that is the same as if someone robbed $15.00 of every $100.00 you currently hold. So when you get a chance write a letter of thanks to president Obama as well as Ben Bernanke, (who is the Federal Reserve Chairman). **Thirdly:** stay away from any and all companies claiming some type of debt relief! While these companies which advertise all the time on television, radio etc. etc. can and will get you out of debt, they accomplish this by charging you hidden fees which can amount to many thousands of dollars. Here is how they all work: you present them with whatever your unsecured debt may be, they then set up an account for you for which they charge stupid amounts of cash for, and then they have you put an agreed amount of capital in that said account each month. They also charge you a fee based upon a percentage of the total debt that you owe, usually 15 to 20 percent! As they say in Brooklyn NY where I was born, Forget about it! All of these companies take advantage of people simply not knowing any better, and you my friend are not going to let anyone take advantage of any situation involving your wealth any more. Look, however you got yourself into debt is in the past, its done. You were smart enough to get this book and start helping regain control of your monetary situation and I am very proud of you. My friend, if you follow the advise which I present in this book you will not only be debt free, you will be changing the course of your life and creating wealth for yourself and your family, and that is a monumental achievement!

Section 14
Let's Start At The End

The American people are taught from a very early age to "follow the status quo, " to be like sheep headed for the slaughter. To be manageable, to think inside the box. I look around every day and observe and what I have seen in my life as an American citizen is a culture today that is destined to fail. In fact if you ask anyone who knows me well enough, I call the American today the "culture of failure."

Look around for yourself, what do you see? Do you see a booming economy, happy, working, prosperous people? I bet you don't. In times past people in this country were entrepreneurial, go getters, who were seeking to improve their situation and that of their families. Today people are looking for a handout any which way they can get it, and that is why social programs in this country exist. Social programs were created to help individuals take control of their lives, not to become dependent on them. These "entitlement" programs have succeeded in creating legions of people who are not able to take care of themselves, and wallow in a pitiful existence because of them. So yes America today on a macro scale is failing because on a micro level the individuals themselves are failures.

Now the fact that you are reading this book proves that you are a winner regardless of how you got yourself into whatever situation you may be in at this moment. So the first order of business is this: I do not want you to blame yourself for getting into debt because in actuality it is not your fault why this happened to you, let me explain: America today is not the land of opportunity; it is the land of debt. In fact our country as a whole is flat broke. America has become the biggest debtor nation on Earth. The monies which are collected in taxes each year does not even cover the day to day expenses of running our country! It covers about 60 percent of them, the other 40 percent must be borrowed in one form or the other.

It is a very sad thing indeed. Also keep in mind that each month America runs a fiscal deficit which increases the national debt, and as such this 60/40 ratio is going to get much worse. Our debt based economy has destroyed our once great nation, and great change is coming in the form of a total global economic collapse. A total global economic collapse is a mathematical certainty and there is no way out of it simply because we have debt based economies globally. Today all we hear about in the news is the European debt crisis, here in America we have a debt issue which eclipses the total of Europe by exponents and this is something which will have to be faced by us all in the not so distant future. Ironically most developed countries today have debt based economies, and it is for this very reason why these crises exist! If there were no debt based economies, sovereign debt issues would never be upon us today. The biggest sovereign debt issue is right here right now in America. The galactic U.S. debt amount will continue to increase by leaps and bounds over the next few years because our policy makers are deliberately causing it to inflate with purpose, and that is to bring about the largest transfer of wealth the world has ever seen. The U.S. debt now accounts for over one hundred four percent of GDP, (gross domestic product). To say that America has a bleak economic future would be the understatement of the century. So let's talk about personal debt, I suppose we all have our own story but here is the truth, you didn't see it coming. Before you knew it you had acquired debt you were unable to pay back, trust me my friend you are not alone. And I will tell you something else, even if you can pay it back don't! There is simply no reason to do it. On a macro scale our country can never pay back the cash it owes to its creditors so why should you? The government keeps giving bailout after bailout to banks and corporations who made bad business decisions so where is your bail out? Oh its coming my friend, don't you worry about that. Let's back up a moment, as you already know our country today is run by what I call the politicocorporatists, that is the policy makers in Washington and the major corporations/investment banks.

Today this merger is more or less common knowledge but no one seems to talk about it. The merger between the government of any nation and corporate powers is defined as Fascism, just like Hitler's Third Reich, and that is the type of government we have today in America. And just like Hitler's thousand year Reich America has a war based economy. Please allow me to explain: Today America has the largest military presence on the planet, with more military bases in more countries than every other country on the Earth combined. The American people have also been forced to fight and die in more military campaigns than every other country on the planet combined, and why do you think this is? Simple: our policy makers will tell you its all to fight the war on terror, *by the way how can you have a war against a noun?* The truth is this, if there was not some type of military conflict many of Americas biggest corporations would not exist, companies like Boeing, General Dynamics, Grumman, Lockheed Martin, etc. etc. all of these companies (and there are many more spanning the globe) are major contributors to our policy makers (Congress and the president) to the tune of billions of dollars each year. So forget the war on terror whatever that is supposed to mean, what we have is a country whose economy is designed to **create debtors**, not wealth, **and war**, not peace. So when I say that you are not a fault for getting into debt, I mean it wholeheartedly. People in America are not taught how to create wealth in school or otherwise, they are told to spend and not save, and why is that? Well Americas debt based economy is driven by consumer spending, in fact over 70 percent of it. If people saved capital, or invested in hard assets like gold and silver the CEO's of the corporations would not be able to reap yearly bonuses in the tens of millions of dollars. Are you also aware that nearly fifty percent of the members of Congress are millionaires as well?

If the Federal Reserve did not issue debt, the central bankers would not be able to create mass private wealth for themselves while at the same time creating mass public debt for everyone else. Understand, there are always two sides to every equation. There are those who will lose and others who will win. The challenge is to get yourself onto the opposite side of the equation as most, and think outside the box.

Yes most people are forced to think inside the box, and that is what makes them more "manageable" for those seeking to take advantage of the situation. See, it all begins and ends with you. It took me a long time to figure this all out but by empowering yourself through knowledge you can easily control your own destiny. Understand, from the very moment you are born there are those who are seeking to direct and control your thought patterns with purpose. Please allow me to explain: society(s) dictate expected patterns of behavior, and these practices begin in the early stages of life which involve the "molding" of our offspring (children) into specific thought processes. At these early stages of life most are introduced into a form of religious belief system, and most often this involves some type of savior deity. Simply, as children we are taught to believe that in order for us to be accepted by God, we have to be "saved" in some way to be worthy of God's grace. So, right from the get go we are taught that we are unable to "stand alone" and are in essence worthless in the eyes of the said God/Deity therefore must be "saved" by accepting and believing in intangible things. Children are taught to understand that in order for them to go to Heaven when they die they must believe in certain things without question. *Now please understand, I am not belittling anyone's religious beliefs and personally I do not care what anyone either believes in or does not believe in, I am just trying to establish how human behavior is caused to happen over time and how this results in a butterfly effect later on in life.*

As we begin to grow we are told that there are other supernatural beings, again which must be believed in, which watch over us throughout the year and if we are good we will be rewarded with gifts at certain times in the year, but if they misbehave they get nothing/punishment. Children now begin to have fear at this point in their life cycle, fear of the wrath of supernatural beings, God(s), unseen things, fright of the dark, etc. etc. Fear is a primal instinct, and it is this emotion which is exploited to the nth degree throughout the human life cycle.

At the most basic level from the very early stages of life free thought is stifled and even frowned upon. Specific patterns of behavior are expected and encouraged with no thought being given to the possible consequences of these actions. So what ends up being created is robots in a sense, an individual who conforms and not a free thinker. All of this now carries on into young adult/teenage life. Parents often get upset at their children for "doing what their friends do," dressing in certain ways, or wanting a particular item because that is what everyone else, has not realizing for a moment that it was they the parents who are responsible for and created these patterns of behavior. So what happens next? Conflict.

The young persons brain cannot understand why now the expected and now ingrained patterns of conformity dictated by society are not being accepted by the parents, and this can lead to depression, anxiety, other health issues, radical behavior, alternative lifestyles, rebellion, drug use etc. etc. As adults again it is society which dictates what you are "supposed to do." All manner of effort is put into causing you to favor this over that, do this and not that, and spend cash, don't save it.

If you live in America today you will notice that you will not see a television commercial advertising for cigarettes, in years past the tobacco industry was allowed to bombard the airwaves with advertisements for tobacco products, not so much today (a good thing I believe). Also in times past you would not see pharmaceutical companies advertising drugs, well today one in every five commercials on average is pushing some type of drug. Today no other country on Earth has more children on some type of prescription drug, adults as well. Today America is the most prescription drug addicted country on the planet bar none. Americans are also the most in debt of all the world's peoples. I suppose it all makes some kind of sense. America is the biggest debtor nation on the planet, so it carries through that the American people would also be the biggest debtors on Earth.
If you were to turn on your television right now chances are that within a few minutes you would see a commercial advertising for some type of financial product like a credit card, some type of loan, reverse mortgage, etc. etc.

We even get offers like these in our mailboxes, spam email, advertisements on billboards, on trains, buses, taxi's, you name it.

Here in the United States one percent of the population controls half the countries wealth, and the vast majority of the people have little or no net worth. The reasons why this is so are simple, we have a debt based economy which is sustained by consumer spending and an incredible amount of effort is placed into keeping the American citizen spending and not saving, in debt and indentured. **When was the last time you saw a commercial advising you to save money?**

There was a time when America was the richest country in the world and the peoples of the world had great envy for those living in this once great country. But today at the hands of our policy makers, the corporate powers, and the military industrial complex, our country and the American people as a whole have been plundered to the point we are at today.

Section 15

America is broke

The United States of America has gone from being the richest country in the world and the greatest creditor nation on Earth, to the biggest debtor nation the world has ever known. America's debt now exceeds its gross domestic product, having hit this mark late in 2011. Although this grim event has historical significance it has gotten almost no media coverage. It must be understood that far and large the American people are sheep, that is their actions and thought processes are caused to happen, institutions of conformity are forced upon us as children as discussed in the previous section and this dictates specific patterns of behavior throughout our lives. It is also for these reasons why it is so difficult for people to think outside the box, and that may be the greatest challenge of them all.

The main stream media news today is filtered prior to being dispersed, and it has been for a while. The information which is distributed is carefully selected as to keep people's perception in check. Today in America with the merger of state and corporate powers perception and not reality by the aggregate public is what matters. Huge amounts of effort is placed into influencing human behavior, from television ads, other types of advertisements, deliberate misinformation, lies, etc. etc. All of this is done with purpose and much of it is to keep you spending and borrowing capital. The greatest lie as of late is the one about our recovering economy being put forth by president Obama and the rest of his administration and parroted by the main stream media. The United States economy is not recovering, it is in fact dying. Ever since the bursting of the housing bubble in 2008 the main driver of the U.S. economic engine has disappeared. Allow me to explain: the housing boom which began in the 1980's was the main facilitator of the U.S. economy.

As we know, seventy percent of the American economy is driven by consumer spending. In the 1980's when the housing boom/bubble began this paved the way for jobs to be created and businesses to thrive. People were making cash, and spending it. Many people took out loans against their appreciating real estate value in an effort to spend even more, and this continued all the way from the mid-1980's until the year 2008. The Dow Jones Industrial Average (DOW) went from 1,500 to over 14,000 during this time, then what happened is this: as in every economic bubble before it, boom! The housing bubble popped leading to devastating losses across the board. The main problem with economic bubbles is not that they form, but the vast majority of the public tend to get in on a rising asset way to late and subsequently hold on the the liability well after the bubble has popped leading to destructive losses. This exact scenario is what has happened to throngs of people who purchased their homes at or near the top of the housing bubble, are you one of them? *Now remember, there are always two sides to every equation, the monies lost by some are collected by others, it does not just disappear.* There are many ways in which cash is made by individuals, and you do not need an asset's price to rise in order to create wealth, in fact more capital is made during an asset's drop in price than is made when the asset it rising. Surprised to hear that? Here is how it works: market forces and asset prices are driven by several factors, and I elaborated at length about these earlier on, but lets review. I will break it down for you in two words, Fear and Greed.

Fear as a driver in an asset's price is actually stronger than greed, and that is why more cash is made when an asset drops in price than when it rises. Let's say a new company is created which makes a product that people want, and let us also assume that this new company is a publicly traded one. This company also has a relatively small "float" of shares it has available to sell. *This "float" refers to the total amount of shares a given company can offer to be sold to the general public.* Now as this company's product is being accumulated its stock price begins to rise rapidly, the media gets a hold of this news and hype begins,therefore stock moves up even higher.

Insiders are already very aware of what is really happening in this scenario, so they as well begin to accumulate shares. Bloomberg, CNBC, and other financial media outlets begin to hype up the meteoric rise of this company's stock and now the general public gets into the action, and a buying frenzy ensues. This asset is now in a bubble having risen beyond what fundamentals, incomes, and economic growth dictate, and the general public has no idea of what is happening, something the insiders are counting on at this point. The aggregate public continue to accumulate the asset, and then-reality sets in and a natural market correction occurs, something the insiders have been well prepared for. For the insiders are well aware way before this correction had occurred that the asset was in a bubble and therefore could not be sustained. So what happens now? Simple. When an asset is rising, "long" positions are taken by traders/investors, that is they are "betting" on the asset's price rising, now, when an asset is falling, these same individuals are again "betting" that the asset's price will drop, and these are called "short" positions. In this manner huge amounts of cash are being made not just on the "long" or up side, but also on the "short" or falling price of the asset. Now don't you believe for a minute that there is a level playing field when it comes to investing and trading assets, the average investor or trader is frankly "dog shit" when compared with the professional. Its like having a farm animal perform neurosurgery, there is simply no comparison. Let me just talk a little more about the bursting of the housing bubble. A home which was purchased at or near the top of the housing bubble is now a toxic asset, and if you can figure a way out of it for example: if you live in a no-recourse state, that is a jurisdiction in which if you decide to walk away from your now toxic real estate asset the lender cannot take legal action against you, simply just walk away. Housing in the United States will never again be in a bubble therefore, homes which were purchased at or near the top of that bubble will never appreciate back up to pre-bubble levels. When an economic bubble pops, that is the end for whatever asset was in that said bubble and the reason why is simple: the driver of the said asset's unrealistic price increase is gone never to return.

When the price of any asset rises above what average incomes and economic growth dictate due to human perception, an asset bubble forms. All economic bubbles must burst because they rise above what can be sustained by any means, there are no exceptions.

Section 16
Break The Chains Of Debt

Just imagine for a moment not owing money to anyone, trust me it is a great feeling and I want you to feel that way all the time. Breaking the chains of debt is freeing yourself from a terrible form of indentured servitude. When we are in debt we become slaves to servicing that debt for years, as well as paying multiples on the initial principal and this my friend is a sure fire way to stay broke for life. Now I am not talking about a home loan, a car loan, or a student loan. Each of these types of loans fall into a totally different type of debt, and these are not necessarily bad. However, I would consider every type of unsecured debt as bad debt in the sense that these types of loans can never create equity/wealth over time, unless of course a loan of this type is used to buy an asset which can be sold for profit. However it is these types of loans (unsecured) which we can easily get out from under, and that is what this chapter is all about! Truthfully I love this stuff, and even if the credit card companies and banks were to offer me cash not to put this information in print I would probably refuse, unless it was a real lot of it I suppose!

I have heard someone say "money is the root of all evil," however I would say being in debt due to the lack of money is the root of all evil. Having wealth is comfortable and I am not going to lie about it. I enjoy having money and being able to acquire assets. People do not need a lot of cash, they just need enough to cover bills comfortably without having to struggle. But not having money enough for your expenses can be devastating across the board.

So what's our plan? Simple. Our plan for getting you debt free involves a straight forward strategy and I am going to begin to outline it for you now. First, I want you to gather all your unsecured debt together, and obtain statements on each of your accounts. I want you to now place them in order from the lowest amount owed to the highest. What we are going to do is tackle the smallest accounts first and I will tell you why.

If you begin to get a handle on this and start to see progress it will be an emotional boost for you. Beginning today you are NOT going to stop paying these bills, what you are going to do is each month send just five dollars to the lender when your bill arrives regardless of what the actual bill is for, and you will do this for all your accounts across the board. This serves two purposes and the first is this: it's a good faith offering to the lender which keeps you from becoming an enemy of that said lender. Keeping a relationship with the lender is important and we will go over why later on. The second purpose in sending the lender a good faith payment is it will keep you out of trouble, what I mean by that is this: if you cut off all communication with a lender and do not at least make a good faith payment, the lender can and often will win a legal judgment against you for the amount of the loan/line of credit in total. If this happens you will then be forced to pay the loan.

If a judgment is won against you in that circumstance, the loan will be either placed as a lien against property you may own, or taken directly out of your paycheck. So let's stick to the plan I am laying out for you. Now, the lenders are not going to like that you are doing this and they will begin to call you in an attempt to get you to increase your good faith payment up to the minimum amount of the bill. Now in truth you do have a choice here and let's go over that now. You can choose to talk to them or not, my advice is talk to them. Explain that you can only afford to pay five dollars a month, do not get angry and keep your cool. Remember I want you to keep a reasonable relationship with them. Some people cannot tolerate the phone calls as you will get them, and they can be very annoying, even harassing. If you really cannot deal with them or if they begin call your place of work you can send them a cease and desist letter via fax and legally they cannot call you after that point. However I want you to try and deal with the calls, and stick to your story that you cannot afford to send them any more. If you cut off all communication with the cease and desist letter it will make it harder for you to deal with the lender later on.

Keeping communication with the lender is a ploy you are using to establish a "working" relationship with the lender which you are going to use to your advantage later on. Now regardless of that, they are going to attempt to scare you with threats of late fees and interest rate increases however do not be intimidated, as long as you stick with this plan they have no recourse and you are in control. The late fees and interest rate increases do not matter **at all,** more on this later on.

Now over the next few months I want you to accumulate some cash, once you have saved about 25 percent of the loan you are going to call the lender and make them an offer to settle the account. If you have done this within six months of beginning this process the loan most likely has not "charged off" yet, that is the lender still owns the loan. If a loan charges off, that means the lender has sold your loan to a collection agency or secondary party who has bought your loan for pennies on the dollar and now you will have to deal with them at that point. It really does not matter who you deal with, either the original lender or the collection agency/secondary party, it will still work out nearly the same for you in the end. If you can work with the original lender before the loan charges off you can often get a better deal, but if you can't you can't, don't worry about it. So whatever time frame you work out, and whether you are dealing with the initial lender or a secondary party you will establish communication and make them an offer to settle the account. Most often you can settle any unsecured debt for 40 percent of the initial loan, any late fees which have accrued will be removed in total as you settle.

Now you may be able to settle these accounts for much less than 40 percent of the principal. I had a $25,000.00 line of credit with Bank of America which I settled for $6,000.00, that's just 25 percent, but on average you will be able to negotiate for 40 percent of the principal. You have other options as well, once you do reach a settlement on the account(s) you do not have to pay them off at that time unless you want to, you have 3 months to do it. So let's say you owe ten grand on account XYZ and you settle for four thousand, (forty percent), you can split this into 3 payments with no fees or interest.

If you have multiple accounts with unsecured debt you can repeat this scenario for each one until you are debt free. Once the lender or secondary party (collection agency) settles with you, you are legally free and clear from any obligation towards the said debt(s) forever ah yes! So you had no idea it was this easy did you? And this is what all those companies who advertise offering "debt relief" are counting on, you not being aware.

Glad I could help!

Now it is time to repair your credit. By getting yourself debt free in this manner and saving yourself enormous amounts of capital, your credit score will be affected negatively but fixing your credit score is a snap to do! Keep this in mind that the credit reporting agency's which are Trans Union, Experian, and Equifax; sole job is to simply collect information and then sell that information to anyone who wants it. These credit reporting agencies do not care if the information which they collect is accurate or not. My advice to you at this point is this: while you can do what I am going to outline next for yourself, consider hiring a reputable credit repair agency and why? Because they are cheap to hire, some as low as $29 dollars a month, and if this is not done properly it can take much longer to repair your credit. On average the credit repair agency's can fix your credit in a year or two at most, if you do this yourself it can take twice that. Here is how it works and again you can do this yourself but I do not recommend it. You obtain your credit report, and this can be done easily via several online sources. If you decide to go this on your own you simply dispute each negative comment which will be placed there by each of the lenders you have settled with. These will show up *as charge offs, settled for less than full amount, late payments, and other negative things*. You simply write a letter to each reporting agency stating that the information is inaccurate. The agencies by law must now investigate your claim and how they do that is this: they contact the said lender to verify whether or not the information is correct, if the agency does not hear back from the lender within 90 days the negative information is removed and your credit score improves. It is that simple. You can repeat this over and over until the negative item is eventually removed.

Now there is a pattern to this, and in order for you to get the quickest result this pattern must be followed and this is where hiring a credit repair agency can be beneficial as they know how to work the system. But before you hire a credit repair agency do a little research online about the agencies performance. Most of the agencies are legit and will help you with repairing your credit and the price they charge is worth what you get out of it. Alright now, one more thing. Come tax time you receive a statement from your now *previous* lenders which will detail your "discharged debt," what this represents is the amount of cash which was removed from your debt. For example: say you had a five thousand dollar balance which was settled for two thousand, Uncle Sam now counts the difference which in this case would be three thousand dollars as income and will tax you on it. Total nonsense right? I agree, but that's the way it is. Still, overall you will have saved yourself thousands of dollars. Heck, maybe I should charge more for this book? What do you think?

Section 17

So Now That You Are Finally Out Of Debt, Now What?

You are going to re-program your brain to think like a successful and prosperous person does, and this is not an easy thing to do because like most Americans since a very early age your thought processes have been hard wired to be average, which is the opposite of successful or prosperous. You're brain has been trained to conform and live your life as the average person does, virtually assuring that you will always remain this-just average. In the past being an average American was not such a bad thing, but today it is a totally different animal. Today forty four percent of the population of the United States receives some type of government assistance and that is just simply ridiculous.

The average person has little or no net worth, and if this person were to lose his or her job at best they could survive 1.5 months off of any acquired savings and this is just pathetic as well. OK, now that you have a straightforward plan to begin taking your life back from the slavery and anxiety of being in debt, you need to develop a picture in your mind of how you want your life to be. Forget about living in the moment anymore, because it was that type of thinking which got you into the situation you're getting yourself out of right now. It is time for you to begin to think long term. Children live in the moment and so do most adults, and that is why so many Americans are in such dire financial condition.

A successful person almost never lives in the moment, their mental world is expansive and is multidimensional. The most simple way to show you an example of how an average and by definition unsuccessful individual goes through life is this: watch the way they walk through a public place. Sounds crazy? Allow me to explain: the average adult walks with their head pointed in one direction with their eyes fixed in one position, rarely looking at anyone or anything, and seemingly oblivious to their surroundings. In contrast, a successful person who by definition is master of his/her domain almost never behaves like this. As he or she walks they are constantly observing, listening, making brief eye contact with other people, perhaps sharing a smile or saying hello to people whom they have never met, getting involved in the situation, even if it just a simple walk.

A successful person is engaged with life and knows how to live it. This pattern of behavior pervades every aspect of a successful person's character and therefore bleeds off into everything they do, and into every person they come in contact with. In order for you to rise above that which society expects of you, *that is be a conformer who simply follows and does not lead,* drastic changes across the board are going to have to be made by you and it all begins with an attitude. You have to purge yourself of decades of being forced into accepting societal dictation on what you are supposed to be, average, and forge your own path towards a lifestyle which you desire to achieve. *The easiest way to start to do this and begin to think "outside of the box" is simple: do the opposite of what the average person does.* For example: when it comes to trading or investing, a professional generally gets in on the opposite side equation, that is if the general public is acquiring an asset or "bullish," the pro is looking to get in on the short side of the trade. And conversely, if the general attitude towards an asset is "bearish" the pro is looking to get into the long side of the trade.

Now keep in mind with financial assets as presented in the scenario above, the pro most likely is taking up positions on both sides of the equation or "hedging" in order to maximize gains while at the same time limiting any possible losses. This situation can also play out with regard to situations in everyday life, that is a rich or successful person does not follow the heard, **ever**. What a prosperous person does is perform the opposite of what is generally expected of them and hedge themselves in order to make the best out of every situation, and this is exactly what you should be doing starting today. Next, learn to observe don't just look at things, focus on them, gain knowledge of whatever it is you are looking at and try to think about why it is that this thing caught your attention in the first place. Observation exercises allow your brain to work independent of conscious thought and after a while of doing this you will be simply stunned as to how such a simple thing, observation, will begin to affect the way in which your brain allows you to process information.

Starting today it is imperative for you to begin to allow your brain to process unconscious thought, and you will do this by simply observing. Next, learn to listen. I do not care how smart you may think you are, in fact if you believe you are smart enough and know more that everyone else the truth is you are probably the stupidest person in the room. Me, I never think like that, I realize clearly that I have a lot to learn from every person I meet and that is the attitude I want you to adapt right now. Once you start to actually listen to people and not just hear them, an entire new world will open up for you. Next, engage in conversation. Engaging in conversation with people once you learn the skills of observation and listening is going to transform you like you cannot believe. Once you can observe and actually listen, each conversation you have is going to be incredibly rewarding for you. I also want you to start asking questions! People today do not want to "look stupid," so they do not ask questions. In my opinion not asking questions is one of the stupidest things anyone can do! An inquisitive person is a thinking person.

Next. Never, and I cannot stress this enough NEVER! Prejudge anyone. A vast percentage of people worldwide have developed a horrid psychological issue, and that is the prejudgment of of people based upon a plethora of things. Think about it for a moment, do you prejudge people? I want you to as of this very moment cease to do that. This type of thinking stifles free thought perhaps more than anything else. It is also this type of thinking which places you at a great disadvantage. By cutting yourself off from others for whatever reason you are not allowing yourself to grow intellectually, and while others are continuing to develop in this manner you will be stagnated. It is you then who will be prejudged by others and thought of as ignorant. People will isolate you, and not want to be involved with you. If you have a particular issue with a specific type of person I want you to consider why that is. Then as an exercise I want you to go out, find a bench somewhere and locate a person or group of people people who fit into your predetermined mental picture, sit there and without being overt about it observe that person/group of people. I then want you to engage in conversation with a person fitting into your predetermined criteria, listen to and know that person.

I know for a fact that after you do these things you are going to shock yourself and understand why I am telling you that prejudgment of a person or class/creed etc. etc of people is not hurting them, it is destroying you.

A successful individual is always seeking to engage and be involved with others at every level and create a persona of approachability, people find themselves drawn to individuals who display these qualities.

Moving on.

After and not before you create this new you so to speak, I want you to again envision how you want your life to be. If you have actually allowed your brain to process unconscious thought by breaking the mold which society has pressed you into, it will be your mind which will lead you on the path of prosperity. Allow me to explain: at this point without conscious thought believe it or not, simply by reprogramming your brain the path to success will be literally laid at your feet. Subconsciously your mind will process thoughts which will direct your actions leading you down a road of happiness and success. Doors which had been closed to you for years, perhaps forever up until this point, will simply open up for you. All this and much more will have all come about by simply altering your conscious thought, which subsequently will allow your unconscious thought to help you achieve your true self.

Section 18

Own

So you want the cheesecake as well don't you? OK, I will give you a taste. *The average American rents, borrows, and leases, his or her way through life and in the end has nothing to show for it.* **That is the definition of how to stay broke, indentured, and miserable.** Let's lay this all out; Renting equals broke; Borrowing equals indentured; And Leasing equals miserable. Any questions? Now as I have been saying, if the average person is doing a particular thing you as a successful person should be doing the polar opposite of what they do and that is OWN things and acquire assets.

Why are rich people rich? They own, it is that simple. I am not going to debate on whether or not now is a good time to purchase a home, but all things being equal the benefits of owning a home greatly outweigh the prospect of renting one. I will elaborate: if you choose to rent you are investing in another persons future, not your own, and every single dollar you put towards renting that property is gone. Conversely, if you owned that same home each dollar used to pay the mortgage is recoverable. That is when the time comes for you to sell your home a large percentage if not all of the monies vested up to a potential profit exist and therefore you have in fact lived in the home for free. Now if that is not a major benefit over renting I sincerely do not know what is.

Rich people rarely acquire unsecured debt, almost never actually, and the only time they lease a vehicle is if it can be written off as a business expense. If you lease a vehicle the scenario is almost the same as if you rented a house, in the end you get nothing but an empty garage. Let's say you purchased a vehicle, car, motorcycle whatever, and the amount borrowed was 30K. An average monthly payment on a loan of this type would be around $650.00 over 4 years. Now let us assume 4 years have passed and you are just tired of the old thing and decide to sell it. Some nice fella comes along and you agree to let it go for 15K.

In essence that vehicle only cost you $325.00 a month because at the end of the loan the vehicle had equity in it. Now, if you had decided to lease that same vehicle for the same term, 4 years, your payments maybe would have been somewhere around $500.00 a month, a bit less however, in the end when you returned the vehicle you would be out the entire amount, $500.00 a month x 4 years. So the new you does not rent, would not even consider borrowing, and laughs at people who lease. Any more questions?

So you want to acquire substantial wealth, OK this is not as hard as you may think it is my friend. The first thing you need to do once you are debt free and have fixed your credit is begin to acquire assets, own things. Obtain a home of your own, buy a car, and obtaining these things is going to be so much easier for you once you liquidate your unsecured debt and improve your credit score as I have outlined for you. So, by definition eliminating your debt burden has paved the way for you to gain real wealth. Having this bad debt off your credit report is also a major boost for you and that will allow you to obtain better terms on any subsequent "good" debt you may acquire. Good debt exists, the kind in the financing of a home for example, or vehicle although to a lesser degree because the vehicle will more than likely depreciate in value, however it will still retain some value. At this point you should also be looking into investment vehicles and there are many.

Afterword
The Path To World War III

The debt crisis now encompassing the world is the prelude to an upcoming much greater juncture, **global war.** All of the pieces are being put into place, alliances are being created between nations, Russia and Iran, Russia and China, Russia and the Middle East. **It seems as if the cold war is starting all over again,** except this time the stakes are even higher. Look around the world, everywhere there is rising tension which seems to get worse with each passing day. Riots, revolt, increasing public anger, saber rattling between nations, and what is the root cause of all this unrest? Sovereign debt, and what is the root cause of the world's sovereign debt? It all has been brought about by nations with debt based economies created by central banks.

It must be understood that any nation which is structured using a fiat monetary system and as such issues debt in the form of fiat not backed by a hard asset is destined to fail over time, there is no way out of it. From the first day a monetary system which is not backed by a hard asset comes into effect, it is doomed to fail and it is simply just a matter of time before a debt crisis like the ones we are seeing now in Europe begins. **Every debt based economy in order to keep functioning must continue to increase it's debt in perpetuity, and once the inevitable point is reached when no more debt can be taken on by that said nation a crisis ensues, this is a mathematical certainty.** It is for this very reason why the monumental debt bubble of the United States will burst in the near future, this event is an absolute sure thing.

Several times in the text I have elaborated on the fact that every economic bubble must burst because they rise above what can be sustained by any means. Historically every economic bubble which has ever formed has burst, there has been no exceptions. Simple math dictates that there cannot ever be an exception to an economic bubble bursting. Once the three pronged debt bubble of the United States begins to burst global pandemonium will ensue.

This one event will change the world greater that any other in human history. Not only is this event going to bring about the largest transfer of wealth the world has ever seen, *as I have elaborated on in the text,* it will also bring about human suffering on a Biblical level. On a macro scale globally normal daily function will cease to exist, grocery stores will be cleaned out and will have no way to be restocked. People will not have access to cash, which will have lost almost all of it's purchasing power by this point. There will be riots in the streets of all nations and many, very many people will die. In the text I present a chart of the population bubble which we are currently in. I believe that this upcoming event is going to cause a major correction in that bubble. Civil unrest will hit epic levels and the already stretched thin military's of the world will be forced to police the streets of every nation, (Martial Law). Somewhere in the world at this point will see the spark which will ignite mass military conflict.

Is there a silver lining to all this? **No.**

Eventually this too will pass and we will rebuild. The corruption, ineptitude, and greed which brought us to this inevitable conclusion will have been replaced by those seeking true peace and justice for all, *and a new cycle will begin.*

Notes

Made in the USA
Lexington, KY
29 March 2013